HUNTER
HALVERSON
PRESS-LLC

2003

Governor
VENTURA
"The Body"
EXPOSED

THE MAN.
THE MANSION.
THE MELTDOWN.

BY DAN CREED

**Four Controversial Years
With an Unconventional Politician.**

| |

DEDICATION

This book is dedicated to my wife, Jan, our children, and all the families of the Residence staff who endured our long hours and long suffering and who supported us through our service to, and recovery from, the Governor Jesse Ventura Administration.

And, to the people of Minnesota.

TABLE OF CONTENTS

FOREWORD

You've heard the expression—Be careful of what you ask for, you just might get it. And boy did we ever get it. What the people of Minnesota asked for when they elected Jesse Ventura as their governor in 1998 was an alternative to politics as usual. Unfortunately, the alternative they got fell far short of voters' expectations for real change. As the manager of the Governor's Residence, I witnessed firsthand just how short of the mark Governor Ventura fell.

I held the top hospitality job in Minnesota, and it was my responsibility to oversee the Residence staff as they served Governor Ventura, his family and the people of Minnesota. The state could not have been better served by our three-and-a-half-years of self-sacrificing service, which we did happily up until the moment the Governor chose to use us to even the score regarding his personal vendetta with the Legislature. For the sake of his own ego, he closed the Governor's Mansion, terminated our livelihoods, and besmirched our personal reputations. The man, who was elected to stick up for the little guy, was the one who stuck it to the little guy. Today, many in Minnesota feel this way, and you will come to know the Governor the way the staff and I came to know him.

All of us learned our employment was to end by watching television news: no warning, no consideration, and no thank you. How politicians survive possessing so little class is often a mystery. Well, sometimes they don't survive it, because even the Governor knew he never had a chance of being reelected.

My regrets are few, and the staff and I have a lifetime bond and friendship through our dedicated service to the State of Minnesota and the treasure trove of stories and experiences that keep us together. I am personally proud of our contribution to the Governor's Mansion. We transformed it from a neglected landmark into Minnesota's premier open-house, worthy of welcoming dignitaries far and wide, the most important being her own citizens.

Nevertheless, I do regret the opportunity Governor Ventura squandered that was entrusted to him by the people of Minnesota—the chance to make a difference. Because I saw it first hand, I have to confess that he did not make a difference because he was incapable of it. He just did not have it within him to deliver on behalf of anyone one else except himself. If it wasn't about Jesse, it wasn't important. Rushing home from the Governor's office each afternoon to faithfully watch The Young and The Restless, rather than reviewing pending legislation, one has to wonder if he did not take his self-proclaimed title of royalty, "Its good to be king," a little too seriously.

In many respects, this is a story about ethics, dignity, and honor betrayed. And, when one distills down the Governor's four years of leadership, it is painfully obvious this story is about a man who was not ready to govern. In his book giving political advice, Do I Stand Alone, he states, "The captain is honor bound to stand by his crew." Well, when the sea became stormy, much by his own making, the Governor threw his loyal crew overboard. In reflection, when it came to governing the people of Minnesota, the Governor gave them the same treatment, and they too, were castaways.

I hope you like some of these stories, many are funny and some outrageous, but they give a brief history of what it was like to be an eyewitness to Minnesota's most flamboyant Governor. And lastly, understand that I feel it is part of my honor bound duty, to myself and "my crew," to stand by the staff in stormy seas, and to set the record straight about the day Governor Ventura chose to close the Governor's Mansion.

SPEEDO DELIVERY!

In the annals of Western Civilization, the course of history has often been changed by the whims of arrogant leaders. Emperor Nero fiddled while Rome was burning; Napoleon sat for a portrait while his troops were surrounded.

In Minnesota, the state budget could not be considered until Governor Jesse Ventura found his missing Speedo.

Governor Ventura didn't get the nickname "The Body" by sitting around. He loves his morning workouts, especially a good swim, and wouldn't know how to start a day without one. Missing a Speedo swimsuit meant not only a workout lost but a personal and gubernatorial shutdown.

On one particularly cold Minnesota morning, staff were busy preparing for the day and awaiting the Governor's departure to the capitol where he had a busy morning of budget meetings.

As I talked to staff in the kitchen, we could hear stomping feet and raised voices coming from the First Family's living quarters upstairs. We knew from experience that the day would not start well for the Governor or anyone in his path.

The problem, we quickly ascertained, was that the Governor could not locate his cherished black Speedo swimming suit. Staff were not immediately concerned because the Governor often misplaced his favorite attire, pen or cigar, all of which were usually located quickly by his more organized wife.

That morning, however, the Governor was on an all-out rage, storming around the mansion, grumbling and growling like a grizzly bear. The First Lady was right on his heels, throwing open drawers and upending the morning in search of the prized black spandex that even she couldn't locate.

Many staff–even those of us who society would implore not to wear such skimpy briefs–were accused by one or both of the Venturas of "moving" the Speedo.

Before long, the First Lady flipped on the mansion intercom and proclaimed to all that, "The Governor cannot go to work today until he finds his Speedo! So, start looking!"

The microphone clicked off, and staff paused in mid-move.

I stopped checking my to-do list with a page half-turned, the chef's spoon stopped stirring and even the First Family's bulldog paused mid-slobber to take in the seriousness of that announcement.

Uff dah! There was no doubt, now, that state business and those morning meetings would have to wait. The gubernatorial Speedo was missing!

Pandemonium exploded as housekeepers took off to look in the hot zone of the family living quarters, and the rest of staff engaged in a hard-target search of the mansion from garbage cans to china cabinets.

Security agents were on the trail in the mansion grounds. Knowing the Governor was apt to forget his golf clubs, paperwork, and even his dog, in his Lincoln Navigator, security searched inside. A flashlight through the rear window finally illuminated a black shimmer wadded in the back of the Ventura chariot.

The Speedo had been left overnight, and it was frozen solid.

After prying the suit from the Navigator carpeting, a security agent scurried inside with the black icicle dangling between two fingers, as if he were trying to run toxic waste through a minefield.

Staff gathered in the kitchen with relief that it had been found but with a growing concern about what to do next.

Did we give the Governor a frozen swimsuit and risk damaging "The Body" when he tried to slip on the ice-encrusted garment? Did we tell the Governor where we found the Speedo, in his own car, thus implying it was *his* fault?

We knew we could do neither.

I had begun to consider an elaborate explanation about Norwegian terrorists trying to steal the Speedo for a clever lutefisk ransom scheme when staff heard the click of the First Lady's footsteps on the stairs. We stood paralyzed, staring at the Speedo that was now standing nearly upright on the kitchen counter.

It's in moments like these that brave souls step forward and risk themselves to save their buddies. That morning that soul was housekeeper Sandy Ellingson.

"We found it! I'll bring it right up!" she yelled.

Then, with catlike reflexes, the brave lass tossed the frozen garment into the Residence dryer and hit the button like Michael Jordan hitting one off the backboard. As if watching James Bond defuse a ticking bomb, staff watched breathlessly as the minutes clicked away. When at last the timer rang, Sandy snatched the steaming Speedo and dashed into the lion's den.

"Sorry for the delay, Governor, but on a cold day like this we thought you'd appreciate us giving it a quick toss in the dryer for you," Sandy offered as she handed Governor Ventura the missing suit.

The Governor took the Speedo with a satiated smile.

Sandy returned to the kitchen with the thumbs-up of a triumphant warrior. She knew, as we did, that we had just spared countless innocent state workers –ourselves included– from a day with a cranky Governor.

The state of Minnesota and its Governor could, at last, get to work.

And, so, we began a typical day in the service of Governor Jesse Ventura.

A frozen Speedo proved to be just the tip of one iceberg in the gubernatorial sea of controversy and comedy through which we Residence staff loyally and skillfully sailed the First Family vessel for three years. What follows are the funny, surprising, disappointing, and true, stories of how we helped keep the official Ventura home afloat, until the Governor himself scuttled the ship.

| CHAPTER 1 |

JESSE: THE PROMISE

The morning after the gubernatorial election in November 1998, my wife Jan and I were sitting in a Northwest jet bound back to Minneapolis from Ibaraki, Japan, where we'd been visiting on a 10-day, Sister City goodwill tour on behalf of the Minnesota Convention and Visitors Bureau.

As we waited for takeoff, the captain announced that Minnesota had a new governor, the long-shot Independent candidate and former professional wrestler, Jesse Ventura. Most of the passengers, including my wife and I, responded with a whisper of disbelief, followed by a loud applause as if to welcome a fresh look for Minnesota politics.

I think CBS TV News Anchor Dan Rather probably expressed the election night shock best. "People could not be more surprised if Fidel Castro came loping across the Midwestern prairie on the back of a hippopotamus!"

After all, this was the upstart outsider who challenged every Minnesota political tradition. He claimed to be a commoner who would indeed represent the average Minnesotan. At times, his off-the-wall approach left traditional politicians speechless, and his Harley riding, boa-wrapping, earring-dangling, bandana attire certainly attracted the young, as well as countless others, from the Minnesota heartland who believed he could represent them.

I began to ponder the new political scene that would greet us back home in Minnesota and tried to imagine how the man I knew only as Jesse "The Body" Ventura would fit into the Governor's office and the traditionally dry committee meetings and hearings held there.

After all, my first exposure to Jesse Ventura was less than gubernatorial. I had been fortunate to get seats close to the floor of a Timberwolves basketball game in Minneapolis' Target Center arena several years before the election. Jesse Ventura was the pregame entertainment. As rock music pumped up our heartbeats, the awed gasp of thousands and a spotlight revealed "The Body" looming high in the rafters. He was poised above us, just a misstep away from certain death. Clad in blue jeans, t-shirt, leather vest and his trademark tough-guy attitude, Jesse took charge of the rope before him in commando style and repelled down to center court.

His mission successful, Ventura bowed to the cheering crowd and walked down the aisle next to our seats. It was obvious that he was a large man, about 6 foot, 4 inches, and 250 pounds. However, even my memory of Ventura's physical stature seemed to shrink a bit as I considered how large he had just become, not only in the state of Minnesota but around the world.

I remembered that I had actually met Jesse Ventura in person once, in the summer of 1998, when I stopped at his Minnesota State Fair campaign booth. He introduced himself, and we chatted briefly. It was apparent from the star struck crowd, wearing Ventura's "Retaliate in '98" campaign t-shirts, that voters were falling in love with the wrestling star's down-to-earth, anti-establishment, commonsense approach to politics. The excitement for Jesse Ventura was certainly building to a frenzied level.

Minnesota had indeed shocked the world when it transformed Jesse "The Body" into Jesse "The Governor." I think it's fair to say that Minnesota, the passengers on my plane and myself were excited at the prospect of stirring up the political pot and shocking the world a little.

In the weeks that followed, news began to circulate about the kind of team this new Independent governor wanted to bring together to run state government. His goal, he stressed, was to have a balanced cross section of all political parties represented. He drew from noted Republicans, Democrats and Independents to fill commissioner and other key government positions.

Many Minnesotans wanted to join in the exciting possibilities for change that Jesse Ventura represented. Thousands submitted resumes to the new administration. Mine was among them.

I was working in special VIP guest services at the four-star Hotel Sofitel in Bloomington when a friend suggested that I apply to be manager of the Governor's Residence because of my strong work ethic, organizational skills and background in the hospitality field, which included my hotel experience and an understanding of international protocol and previous residence management experience in the home of a university president.

In early January, 1999, I was invited to an interview with the chief of staff, Steven Bosacker, and the First Lady, Terry Ventura. While, traditionally, Residence positions such as housekeepers and chefs remain through changes in administration, the manager, assistant manager and First Lady assistant positions were usually newly hired by each incoming administration.

As I waited for my interview in the foyer of the Governor's office, Mrs. Ventura came through the door. I was instantly taken by her beauty, grace and charm. She was tan and physically fit from years of horseback riding and walked with an elegant confidence. We made eye contact and said hello. Later, Terry told me that she had hoped the kind-looking man in the lobby was the one coming in for the interview.

When I entered the office, the Governor was already there. Again, I was taken by his presence.

There is a certain instant appeal about Jesse Ventura, and I felt it again the moment I met him. Most people naturally look up to him because of his size, and he is charismatic, especially on stage. He portrays a confidence in himself and his opinions that makes you want to cheer on his side.

Jesse Ventura didn't just look like a hero; he was a hero. Long before he became Governor, he had been a hometown boy made good, a Vietnam veteran, an athlete, a movie star, an icon. And now he was the underdog who beat the system, the political grassroots winner who you just wanted to get behind.

The minute I met him, I wanted to like him; I really did. I think everybody feels this way, initially.

Though the Governor sat in briefly on our interview, my hire was ultimately the First Lady's decision, so Terry Ventura asked all the questions. Most centered around her family, especially around the Venturas' two teenage children, son Tyrel and daughter Jade. The First Lady was most concerned about how staff and I would deal with Jade because she was both a young adolescent student and a special needs child. When I conveyed to Terry that I also had a teenage daughter who was similarly situated, the First Lady seemed relieved and immediately stood up and gave me a hug.

Terry Ventura and I hit if off from the start, but then, Terry got along instantly with everyone who met her. She insisted from the first we call her "Terry," a stark contrast from the Governor, who was always addressed as "Governor," even by his wife when they were in public.

Everybody was enamored with the Governor's greatest asset, his wife. She was, and is, sweet, beautiful and, for the most part, very caring. She has that kind of appeal that you just naturally wanted to take care of her, protect her, go so far as to take a bullet for her.

The concerned wife and mother I met that day also wanted assurance that I would be able to transform the large Governor's Residence into a home. I conveyed to her that even though the house was an official state building where important business was conducted on behalf of the people of Minnesota, by adding the right touches and amenities, it could easily be made comfortable.

I thought that my interview went well, and I grew even more eager about the job, and about working for the Venturas, when Terry called several times with follow-up questions.

A few days after the interview, I got the call I wanted. Steven Bosacker offered me the position as Residence manager and asked me to report for work the following Monday. My wife and I were elated!

I called, literally, every one I knew and even announced my new job at church where I took some good-natured ribbing from fellow parishioners about how I was putting myself so close to "The Body." I took my family out to dinner to celebrate, and they shared in my excitement about being offered what I considered to be the top hospitality job in Minnesota.

A POSITION OF PRIDE

Our euphoria echoed much of Minnesota's sentiments, which seemed to crescendo as I joined the thousands welcoming the new governor to office at the Ventura's inaugural celebration Jan. 16, 1999.

One of the first glimpses of how the new governor differed from previous state chief executives was offered by the not-so-ordinary celebration of his election victory. Instead of the usual Governor's ball, Jesse Ventura hosted a party for the Minnesotans who elected him. He called it, "The People's Celebration."

The people certainly celebrated. A real party flavor once again saturated the Target Center that evening as 14,000 celebrants packed into the arena. Beer flowed and excitement built as the faithful wandered the corridors before the victory show, enjoying a variety of food and singing, clapping and shouting to music performed by 12 bands. Fans and supporters were stacked in three-deep throngs near the stage, creating a screaming bulge of humanity the like of which I hadn't seen since The Beatles invaded American pop culture.

A *Harper's Magazine* reporter described the crowd as "thick of neck and stout of heart … all white and worked up." The Ventura masses certainly painted that picture with a broad brush stroke, but from my vantage point inside the throngs, the victorious scene was filled with Minnesotans from every walk of life, including professionals, blue-collar workers, motorcycle bikers and especially young people, dressed in everything from leather biker vests and cowboy hats to evening gowns, tuxedoes and a lot of Minnesota Viking purple.

As we waited to take our seats, a local newspaper reporter was asking people why they had dressed as they had. I was wearing a business suit and he asked me why. I explained that I had come straight from church and was going to work for the new governor and wanted to set a good example.

The Governor I was going to work for was much less concerned about his appearance that night than I was about mine.

In classic Ventura style, the First Family arrived via motor coach from the Governor's Residence, escorted by state police and an entourage of motorcycle bikers. The new Governor's attire was certainly not typical gubernatorial dress. He donned a tan, fringed leather jacket, red and white head bandanna, earring, sunglasses and his trademark pink boa. The crowd went wild with cheers and applause when the Governor was escorted into the building.

Entertainment included the legendary Delbert McClinton, Johnny Lang and Warren Zevon. The Governor got into the act and sang several tunes with Warren Zevon. The Governor had invited members of the '70s rock band America to the party to play their Dewey Bunnell hit, "Ventura Highway." The song is one of Jesse Ventura's personal favorites from his California and early college days. It was a hit song about the time that the then James George Janos was looking for a wrestling name and opted for Ventura, the California highway America sings about, which he cruised during a brief stint in a California motorcycle gang. Besides the title, some of the song's lyrics obviously spoke to the flamboyant new Governor we were celebrating that night. As the crowd cheered, Jesse Ventura joined the band in belting out those lyrics:

...Wishin' on a falling star
Waitin' for the early train
Sorry boy, but I've been hit by purple rain
Aw, come on, Joe, you can always
Change your name
Thanks a lot, son, just the same

Ventura Highway in the sunshine
Where the days are longer
The nights are stronger than moonshine
You're gonna go I know

'Cause the free wind is blowin' through your hair
And the days surround your daylight there
Seasons crying no despair
Alligator lizards in the air, in the air...

The Governor and crowd also joined in while the band played "A Horse With No Name," a favorite of the First Lady, an equestrian businesswoman who ran a horse ranch operation.

Though the inaugural crowd loved watching their rebel politician get up and rock with the band, many of us fans were glad that the singing Governor had a day job.

During the show, I had the opportunity to sit next to a biker and his girlfriend. He could not stop talking about how great the next four years were going to be with "The Body" as Governor. He was confident the newly elected Governor would do many things to help the average citizen. He certainly echoed the hopes and sentiments of Minnesotans who packed the Target Center that evening.

Like most Americans, this man and many Minnesotans like him had been ready for a change from traditional politics, and Jesse Ventura was change personified. Voters were tired of the affairs and impeachment of Bill Clinton, they felt betrayed by former President George Bush's promise of "no new taxes," and they were frustrated by politics as usual from the usual cast of characters. A national Reform Party had already ridden this tide to contender status in the most recent presidential election when Ross Perot caught many voters' attention.

Added to this change fervor was Minnesota's traditional unpredictability as a state that consistently turns out 20 percent more voters at the polls than the national average and whose voters have rallied behind such fiery political mavericks as Senators Eugene McCarthy and Paul Wellstone and Great Depression-era, Farmer-Laborite Governor Floyd B. Nelson. The state is perhaps the only one in the union to have elected two minority-party candidates in a row, as it did in the 1930s according to an Oct. 21, 2002 *USA Today* article. Minnesota has even elected a third-party governor once before when voters chose Silver Republican Party candidate John Lind to lead the state more than 100 years ago, reports Jacob Lentz in *Electing Jesse Ventura*.

Minnesota's taste for political change had yet to be satiated when Jesse Ventura threw his bandanna into the gubernatorial ring in 1998. Minnesota was always open to something different, and the cheering Target Center crowd welcomed the change for which they had voted.

The native son echoed the hopes of those eager voters in the welcome he wrote to guests. "So why 'The People's Celebration,' you ask? I say, 'Why do the same old Governor's Ball in the same old way?' This event is not about recognizing me, but rather about honoring you. You are the people who placed a strong faith in my election and my promise to you is to do the best I can. The time for serious change is long overdue: change accomplished through bold dreams and hard work."

THE PEDESTRIAN TOUR

My hard work for the dream began two days later when I reported for duty as the new manager of the Governor's Residence.

Monday, January 18, 1999, Martin Luther King's birthday, was a typical, snowy Minnesota day. As I neared the mansion at 1006 Summit Avenue in St. Paul, I was struck by how majestic and massive it looked in the snow. Built in 1910 by lumber baron Horace Irvine, the red stone English Tudor-style mansion was donated to the state in 1965 by Irvine's daughters Clotilde Irvine and Olivia Irvine Dodge, the last owner and private resident of the home. The Irvine home was the state's first official Governor's Residence and, since then, six governors had lived there. I was charged with making this stately Residence into a home for the seventh.

As I drove toward the gate, I wondered how staunch Republican Horace Irvine and his passionately Democratic wife, Clotilde, felt about their new Independent houseguest.

When I arrived, a groundskeeper was plowing the front drive. I asked if I could come in and, to my surprise, he said, "Yes, you are the boss." The role of Residence manager was only beginning to sink in.

I first went to the carriage house, located over the garage, which houses the staff offices. It was a nice suite of rooms, but it sorely needed some organization. Upon closer inspection, I realized all of the filing cabinets were empty. For some reason, all hard copy and computer files had been removed, thus eliminating vendor lists, phone lists and other vital information. There were no records of previous functions or billing systems or even a calendar of upcoming events. Apparently, in political rivalry tradition, someone in the previous administration had purged the files.

The Venturas had not yet moved in, and because it was a holiday, no staff was on duty inside the 16,000-square-foot house that Horace built.

As I walked up the red carpet, I drank in the mansion's grandeur in silent splendor. I felt a bit like a parent looking in love, awe and trepidation at his newborn for the first time. In many ways, this Residence was Minnesota's child, and I had been entrusted to look after her.

I entered into the main level foyer through two sets of double doors enhanced by beveled glass and wrought iron grillwork. This is where guests are received by and wait for the Governor.

Guests are awed, as I was, by the richness of the oak wood in the main foyer, showcased by the soft light from beautiful crystal sconces on the walls and accentuated by a large, crystal chandelier and a grand staircase that leads up to the Governor's private quarters. As I toured, I noted that the First Lady—who, like me, was getting used to the new surroundings that week—had already added a Ventura touch to the foyer by hanging several horse paintings along the staircase.

It was hard to believe that in the early 1980s the rich oak had been bleached blond. Thankfully, the wood was restored and an antique Oriental rug replaced yellow, wall-to-wall carpet.

A six-foot, 17th Century, Scottish clock towers along one foyer wall while several settees (benches) and two high-back European chairs—covered in Ostrich hide and beginning to show their wear—rest nearby. A large weathered chest also caught my eye, as it does many a visitor's. This showpiece was the beautiful hiding place for the buffalo robes that the Irvines wore when driving around in one of Minnesota's first horseless carriages.

Two steps down, I entered the spacious, sunlit solarium, located on the south side of the house. The only room added after the house was built, the solarium features the warmth of a wood burning fireplace and the flexibility of four, tall glass doors that open onto the terrace, providing easy guest flow in and out of the house and gardens. Just off the terrace, I could see a fountain with two statuettes, produced from the same foundry in France that produced the Statue of Liberty. I soaked in the beautiful setting and smiled knowing that our solarium guests would have good historical company since former First Ladies of the United States Eleanor Roosevelt and Hilary Clinton both had tea in this room.

Stepping up two steps to the west I found the formal dining room where the paneled walnut walls match the arched ceiling panels. I noted the dining table extends to seat 18 guests comfortably in an antique enhanced décor that featured such treasures as White House-style knife boxes for diners to use.

A sliding door led me across a hallway to the mansion's cozy yet elegant library where a collection of novels, including a signed book by Mark Twain, is well preserved. A 17th Century women's crystal cordial set, an English butler table and a land-lord's circular renters table complete the historical atmosphere. Thickly padded, white-paneled walls showcase a large painting of Minnesota's first governor, Henry H. Sibley riding a horse. It's titled, what else? "Sibley on Horseback."

I crossed the foyer again and entered the drawing room where an elegant backdrop of mahogany is highlighted by 17th Century antique furnishings, a large collection of Japanese Imari pottery, 12 to 15 paintings donated from local art muse-ums and a tired looking Steinway grand piano—in need, I noted, of tuning. The combination would provide a richness and warmth for both family gatherings and stately official meetings.

I knew that, traditionally, the First Lady chose the donated art for this room—a special draw for guests who are always eager to see what theme and which artists the First Lady select-ed from local galleries. (For example, one year Terry Ventura chose works by Minnesota artists.) It would be my duty to ensure that the donated art was properly cared for and protect-ed, and I felt particularly privileged to be entrusted with such a priceless responsibility.

I traveled downstairs into additional rooms, including a com-fortable, burgundy-colored family room equipped with large screen television and a donated billiards table, a large coatroom, two public bathrooms and a conference room that housed two of the oldest furnishings in the mansion, a 16th Century Italian settee and a Scandinavian armoire dated 1764.

The basement conference room, called "The First Lady's Room," displays photos of all of the First Ladies, dating back to territorial days, along one of its marble dust-covered walls. Photos of the Irvine family are spotlighted on another wall.

Finally, I took a peak at the First Family's living quarters on the second floor where there are three bedrooms and a small liv-ing room. The Governor's bedroom, where the Mrs. Irvine gave birth to three daughters, is the largest. The room also features a comfortable sitting porch and, as I stepped into it, I could almost see Mrs. Irvine standing there, soothing a crying newborn as she crossed its sturdy timbers in the wee morning hours.

Looking outside from the second story, I could easily view the Children's Garden on the back lawn, a site inspired by

Terry's predecessor, First Lady Susan Carlson, on a trip to the White House during which she toured a similar garden developed by First Lady Jackie Kennedy and dedicated to all children who lived in the White House. Today, the names of the 20 children who've called the Minnesota Governor's Residence home are visible along the pathways of Mrs. Carlson's garden.

Also visible is the Man-Nam statue on the west side of the front lawn, erected to honor all Minnesotans killed in the Vietnam War. Designed by Minneapolis native Paul T. Granlund, this tribute was dedicated by First Lady Lantha LeVander September 27, 1970.

While venturing about that first morning, I also discovered a quick escape route for future use, a secret passage built between the carriage house and the Residence. Though a disconcerting walk for the claustrophobic, the narrow utility tunnel not only provides dry access on wet days but ample opportunities to startle coworkers by turning out the lights when they are halfway to the other side!

A NEW TO-DO

I was certainly awed by the splendor of the mansion that first day, but I must confess that I was shocked by the state of the Residence and its furniture.

As a proud Minnesotan, I was angry to find, for example, that carpets were threadbare and furniture desperately needed reupholstering or repair. Many of the crystal sconces in the foyer were missing globes, several Oriental rugs were especially threadbare, and outside lighting was scarcely ample enough to light one's way, let alone illuminate flagpoles in dignity.

I had toured the White House in Washington, D.C., years before and had expected that Minnesota would have kept its house up to the same standards. There was, sadly, no comparison that first day. With every turn, I noted much restoration work needed to be done. And, I discovered many a state treasure, including antique silver pieces, tapestries and dishes, stuffed haphazardly in attic boxes to be forgotten and destroyed by time. For example, in one tattered box, I found several tarnished silver pieces, including a soup tureen and a pair of candleholders, which we eventually re-silvered and set to work in the dining room. In another box, I uncovered a 200-year-old tapestry that was later restored to become a foyer wall hanging.

Surely, our grand old lady deserved better treatment, and I began to feel that part of my job would be to try to rescue the state's treasures and the house that held them for the people of Minnesota.

Beyond obvious repairs, the Residence also needed some organizing. Residence furniture and treasures, I soon discovered, were stored at the capitol, in the attic and in every nook and cranny. As staff came on board, we organized every drawer, cabinet and storage area and boxed and labeled items to store or dispose of them in a proper manner.

As I learned and developed the details of the job, I wrote them down. I was determined that when I left this position, a new manager would have a complete manual to follow instead of empty file cabinets. The manual I subsequently wrote, *How To Operate a Governor's Residence*, was the thesis of the master's degree in organizational management I earned during my tenure as Residence manager.

Though I noted many needed repairs that first day, I knew the mansion had the treasures it did thanks to the tireless efforts of the Governor's Residence Council (an overseeing body appointed by each governor) and the 1006 Society (a fund-raising organization for the benefit of the residence), as well as several private donors. Because of their donations and efforts, valuable furnishings have been saved and added over the years to complement the elegance and stateliness of the Residence.

For example, the Governor's Residence Council had a $4.6 million Master Plan for the mansion when I arrived. It included major structural and safety improvements such as adding an additional stairway from the second to third floor, taking the elevator to the second and third floors (it currently only goes from the basement to the first floor), creating a guest suite of rooms on the second floor, adding a hallway on the second floor, installing central air-conditioning, redesigning the kitchen for greater meal preparation space and updating an advanced security office.

With all those cosmetic changes to plan for, and my main job to handle—that of hiring and overseeing the residence staff, coordinating all mansion events and finding a comfortable way for the people's house to serve as the First Family's home—there was little doubt that I had embarked on a challenging job. I was honored that Minnesota had entrusted me with such responsibility, and I could hardly wait to get started!

A LOYAL STAFF

Job one was learning where all the light switches were!

As soon as I could "see the light," I set about organizing the mansion and building the right team to serve the Governor, his family and the Residence. In short order, I was able to add to the previous administration's carryover staff of two chefs and housekeepers and assemble a dedicated bunch who brought individual expertise, personality and a fun and harmonious attitude to the gubernatorial workplace.

Our French trained chefs, **Ken Grogg** and **Nate Cardarelle,** loved their kitchen almost more than their lives, or so it seemed to any errant pantry visitor who stumbled upon them in the midst of a gourmet creation. The two earned rave reviews from all who dined at the Residence, and we knew that Minnesota's finest hotels couldn't possibly keep up with Ken and Nate's culinary speed and caliber.

The artistic duo especially enjoyed developing creative entrees to please and surprise the First Family and their guests. Terry is a vegetarian—except when it comes to lobster—who loved the special corn casserole our chefs prepared for her. The Governor is no vegetarian. If he ate a salad, it would only be as a means of getting to the main course. Still, our chefs kept trying to get the Governor to eat his vegetables by sneaking a piece of spinach onto his plate or disguising veggies with sauce. Despite their best-intended efforts, the Governor's plate would return empty, save for a lonely green slab of nutrition.

Though the meat-and-potatoes Governor enjoyed everything from walleye to rack of lamb, he did have a favorite. Jesse Ventura devoured the chef's meatloaf and requested it often. He learned, however, never to ask our chefs for his favorite condiment, ketchup! In all his wrestling days, I doubt "The Body" ever encountered a look as deadly as one chef shot the Governor when he first asked for the "cheap red sauce."

Administrative Assistant **Sylvia Sanchez** stepped into her organizational role as office chief and Residence mother with equal doses of General Patton candor and Roseanne Barr humor, a combination that always kept us wondering—and sometimes worrying—what she would say next. This grand-mother of 10 is as quick with advice as she is with a warm hug, always knowing which to dish out just when you need it. She is equally at ease with dignitaries and tour groups, and it never took long for a guest to get to know and remember Sylvia—and even comment weeks later about her warmth and charm. When we hired Sylvia away from the capitol where she was answering phones, she told me that both she and her mother, who lives with her, cried with joy at the idea that the daughter of Mexican immigrants would be working in such an important and prestigious place.

Assistant Residence Manager **Cassandra Yarbrough** is a beauty both inside and out. Cassandra appeared so perfectly put together no matter how hard it was raining or how many hours we'd been at work that we nicknamed her "princess" and often kidded her about typing because she might break one of her manicured fingernails. In reality, our princess is anything but high and mighty. She is extremely professional, a proficient typist and a hard worker who would stop at nothing—from changing light bulbs to chasing rats—to get the job done. Cassandra joined us about six months into the administration from the capitol staff pool and was especially excited about working at the mansion since she grew up four blocks away and spent her childhood dreaming about what it would be like to be inside. Her imagination especially ran wild on Halloween when she'd venture to the spooky gates for treats.

Our housekeepers **Jean Klucas**, **Sandy Ellingson** and **Beth Karlisch** held the mansion together and kept us all in stitches. The diligent trio was continuously looking for ways to improve the appearance of the Residence and took on such challenges as polishing every brass item in the house from doorknobs to bed frames. Sandy has a true gift for room aesthetics and was especially concerned with making the mansion shine. She would call me so often at home with ideas for better furniture arrangements that I accused her of dreaming about the Residence. Jean, who came to us from the previous administration and stayed the first year, was my source for much of how the Residence operated in the past. I never would have found most of the light switches without her.

We started calling Sandy and Jeane "Laverne & Shirley" because they were a fun-loving duo who always had great stories to tell. Housekeeping knew the Venturas more intimately than most staff ever wanted to. After all, these women cleaned the Governor's bathroom several times a day, picked up after his teenage children, followed his wife's wishes and, yes, washed and folded the gubernatorial underwear. Talk about "airing" dirty laundry!

Steward **Theresa "T" Finnegan** wins the staff Miss Congeniality award hands down. Theresa has a genuine beauty only enhanced by her inability to ever say a bad or dishonest word about anyone. She was closest to the Venturas on a personal level as the staff member most requested to tend the family in private settings and at events in their Maple Grove home. The Governor even remembered and used her first name and often introduced Theresa to his friends when she was serving snacks during a televised ball game or out at the Venturas' home. As steward, Theresa arranged food service and maintained all service equipment such as silver pieces, china, glassware and flatware. Her job was an amazing amount of work for one person considering that polishing all of the Residence's silver pieces was a full-time job by itself.

Theresa's work at the Residence extended far beyond her official job description. In addition to pitching in whenever and wherever needed, Theresa is a talented chef in her own right and often cooked the Governor's meals and snacks when our chefs were off duty. She is also quite artistic, and her elegant and elaborate floral settings and buffet arrangements were the center of attention. I personally tracked her down at the Hotel Sofitel, where we'd both worked, to offer her the job. It took a bit of convincing because she thought I was teasing her at first, but I assured Theresa that I could think of no more talented, professional or gracious steward to hire.

Groundskeeper **Bill Suchy** is indeed a down-to-earth man who was such a soft-spoken soul that we took to calling him our Gentle Giant. Bill is not only an expert gardener and landscaper but a willing worker ready to move furniture, set up banquet tables and clean up. He is considerate and compassionate toward others and always made sure there were fresh flowers on everyone's desk. He fed the gubernatorial squirrels corncobs and cut fresh flowers for tourists who needed a smile.

Bill has a dry sense of humor that sneaks up on you after a beat or two and is the kind of guy who hangs one of those singing fish "trophies" in his office. Every time he would clap, or someone would speak too loudly, that rubber fish would start talking. We all still laugh about the night one of the Residence security men actually drew his gun on the fish—as it spouted "let me out of here"—when the bass went off in the dark as he was checking rooms. We're happy to report that the fish "lived" to sing another tune.

Though security remains none too fond of Bill's unusual office décor, everyone enjoys the picturesque beauty of the grounds he created. Bill did such a terrific job planning and maintaining the 1.5-acre gardens—including planting and replanting 3,000 tulip bulbs a year—that we often bragged, "We work in paradise." Though changing annual color schemes and keeping the premises pristine was time consuming, Bill's work was a labor of love.

Bill poured much of himself into the Residence. We all did. I can say with certainty that the Residence staff came into the Ventura administration excited to be helping this maverick Governor fulfill his dreams for the state. We were all caught up in the dream and determined to do our part in making the Governor and the state great.

As the people poised to witness some of the most intimate moments of the Venturas' home and state life, we further strove to meet the First Family's personal needs and tastes and do all that we could to make the state mansion feel more like their home.

We learned, for example, to always stock the freezer with DiGiorno® pizza and ice cream sandwiches, the Governor's favorite snacks. Preparing the Governor's morning protein shake was the first order of business for housekeepers, after turning on the lights. And, we never served the Governor coffee. Governor Ventura did not take any caffeine and rarely drank alcohol. He preferred Pepsi Free® at every opportunity, and we learned to pour just a ounce of wine into his glass to give guests the appearance he was joining them. If Jesse Ventura drank alcohol, it was Bombay Sapphire® gin and then only with friends and special guests. He preferred it only straight or on the rocks, a surprise for a flamboyant wrestler who seemed more the Pink Bombay & Tonic or Cowboy Martini type. Staff also noted that daughter Jade was a big fan of those nonalcoholic Shirley Temple cocktails, and we tried to bring one to her at every special event.

Staff viewed such details as the stuff of doing a good job. After all, our mission was to serve the Governor and First Family and, at all times, make them look their best to their guests, to the guests of the state of Minnesota.

FIRST FAMILY MOVES

Those first weeks of service at the Residence were a "rose-colored glasses" affair indeed. Staff, family, and even the media, were caught up in the happy honeymoon of all that the Ventura administration promised.

It was early into the honeymoon that I first met the Venturas' two children. I liked the kids right from the start and, naturally, came to feel protective of them. Then 15, Jade is, a determined young lady whose strength and stamina is disguised by a Grace Kelly graciousness. She is a sweet and beautiful person. Jade was born with seizures caused by a rare B6 deficiency and takes daily doses of the vitamin. Suffering a slight speech impediment, Jade is mainstreamed in school and excels in both horseback riding and piano playing. I, and the rest of staff, truly enjoyed looking after this enchanting sprite, who always had a smile for us.

Tyrel, then 18, has his parents' strong-willed independence, sense of humor, intelligence and his father's love of the limelight. As a recent high school graduate, the Ventura's elder child went from homeroom to the Governor's Mansion and lived there more than any other member of the family. Tyrel was driven by a passion for filmmaking, and little else. His room was always stuffed with videos and magazines pertaining to the movie business. The Ventura son even dressed dramatically, favoring a morose, all-black appearance or flashy disco-style shirts the likes of which haven't been seen much past the dance floor at Studio 54. The garb fit so well with Tyrel's late-night arrivals and late-morning sleep-ins that the security group nicknamed him "the vampire."

As I got to know the Venturas on a personal level day to day, I came to see and respect the strong marriage and commitment to family they enjoy. Anyone who worked with the Venturas would echo their proud, protective and even defensive support of each other and of their children.

The Venturas met in 1974 at a Twin Cities bar where Jesse Ventura was a bouncer. As the story goes, Terry and some friends walked in and she was instantly taken with the handsome body builder with pro-wrestling dreams. His long, blonde locks reminded her of wrestling superstar Billy Graham, who she liked to watch on Saturday nights before going out. Terry confessed once to me that it was love at first sight.

While the Governor was never one to express such sentiments publicly, he did sweetly detail just how taken he was with the Minnesota native in his autobiography, *I Ain't Got Time to Bleed.*

"She walked in (to the bar) and our eyes met. Her eyes were so beautiful. I had to know who she was ... I was thinking, 'God, what do I say? I have to say something to her and I can't just let her walk on by.'"

I often chuckle at the thought that the Governor couldn't think of something to say. After all, I never knew Jesse Ventura to be speechless about much.

Neither did I think, at first, that he was the kind to shy away from confrontation, which is why I was really surprised to learn that he proposed marriage over the phone. Terry accepted, and they wed nine months after their first meeting, on a summer evening in 1975.

When I first started to work for them, the Ventura's marriage had held strong for nearly 25 years, through a poor start in the wrestling business, through his near death from a pulmonary embolism and through the birth of a special needs child who spent 60 days in intensive care.

The Venturas tease each other, work out and have fun together, are proud of each other's accomplishments, and certainly stand up for each other no matter what.

Terry very much adores her husband; you can see it when she looks at him. I think that, deep down, Jesse Ventura knows that his wife is his greatest asset. He will often bend to his wife's wishes and sometimes do what he detests just to please her. Terry may be the only person who can get away with telling Jesse Ventura what to do. I can think of few better examples of this than to describe one of the personal changes the Venturas made to the Residence shortly after they moved in.

While I made tremendous efforts to restore the mansion to its authentic historical state, Terry proceeded in a different direction and painted the master bedroom, of all colors, pink! I kept my mouth shut, but it was not easy since my lips kept flopping open whenever I passed by the Pepto-Bismol walls, trimmed in cough syrup fuchsia and highlighted by a flowery bedspread.

Many visitors commented that they couldn't imagine Jesse "The Body" sleeping in a pink bedroom, but he did! (I have since learned that Ventura's successor, Governor Tim Pawlenty did not move into the mansion until those walls had been repainted in shades of cream.)

Perhaps apropos, Governor Ventura also slept in a 1970s throwback waterbed. Not only was it unusual, but the bed was a bane to the maintenance crew. It seemed to spring leaks at inconvenient times.

The combination of strange colors and furniture seemed to me to be more representative of the places the Governor would later brag that he visited in Las Vegas. There were only a few reminders that a former wrestler slept here scattered within the feminine landscape, but a few movie and wrestling photos did make the fashion cut.

The Governor's most recognizable possession was carefully looked after, however. His infamous matching pink boa was often placed carefully in the closet along with his fringed leather jackets. Occasionally, we'd find the boa lying on top of the bed or hung across a chair. That boa, to this day, still unnerves me for reasons I can't really put my finger on.

The Venturas' bedroom turned out to be more than an interior design showplace, at least for one Residence neighbor. When we first arrived, the bedroom's north wall had electronic pullback drapes but no shades. A neighbor across the street registered an embarrassing protest with staff that the Venturas' bedroom curtains were ALWAYS open! Apparently they saw more of "The Body" than they cared to. Fortunately for the neighbor and everyone else concerned, staff had just ordered the bedroom window shades that week. No more complaints were heard.

With an introduction like that, the stage was certainly set for a different kind of gubernatorial performance at 1006 Summit Avenue. The flamboyant governor's popularity ensured that the stately mansion we all just moved into would play host to a cavalcade of Hollywood celebrities, dignitaries and questionable characters from around the world. From this dramatic platform the entertainment icon called "The Body" would attempt to govern.

CHAPTER 2

JESSE: THE HOST

Into Governor Ventura's ring walked some of the most famous, revered and celebrated guests in Minnesota and beyond. When you could get Jesse Ventura onto the stage, he relished being the center of attention, and he was good at it. He was charismatic, funny and charming—a most memorable host to be sure.

Never was the Governor in better form than when Hollywood came to visit.

The Governor's Residence first welcomed movie stars to the Ventura spotlight Feb. 24, 1999, when Jack Nicholson and Sean Penn joined the Governor and Mrs. Ventura for dinner after a day of scouting a Minnesota location for their movie, *The Pledge*. The dinner invitation had been extended, and paid for, by the Minnesota Film Board to help boost the state's chances for selection as the filming site. Though the night was the Venturas' first official celebrity dinner, it was not the first time Hollywood had visited Minnesota. The mansion entertained many celebrities even before the Venturas moved in, including the cast of the movie, *Grumpy Old Men*, while it was filming in Minnesota. Dinner guests then included Ann-Margret, Walter Mathau, Burgess Meredith and Jack Lemmon.

The Ventura's first Hollywood night was a needed change of pace for the First Family, who had just returned from National Governors Conference meetings in Washington, D.C. The local media had not been particularly complimentary in coverage of the trip, despite a gracious national press. The Governor and First Lady were both a hit in the U.S. Capitol. Terry looked especially beautiful in the photos taken at the White House dinner, and the Governor appeared in fine form on several talk shows while he stormed Washington, D.C. He made a grand, Ventura-style entrance at the conference as well, schmoozing with other politicians in his buckskin jacket.

The star-studded evening proved both interesting and exciting. The guests of honor arrived in a limousine, pulling up under the portico. It was my pleasure to greet them and escort them inside to meet the First Family.

Word leaked to the media about the dinner, and the usual hordes of reporters were camped outside in spite of the cold weather. One television station even called my home number and asked my wife to find out what was being served. When I asked the First Lady if she cared to respond, she said to tell them we were having meatloaf and mashed potatoes. Actually, we served rack of lamb.

A staff debate of sorts had ensued over which star should be seated to the Governor's right, the highest place of honor. After discussion with the Governor, we placed Jack Nicholson in the top seat because of his seniority status in Hollywood; Sean Penn sat to the Governor's left. The Governor had a lot of fun with this from that night forward and would often tell guests that they were sitting in Jack Nicholson's or Sean Penn's chair. Interestingly, the Governor never referred to the chairs as anyone else's, even though the Crown Prince of Norway and U.S. Vice President Al Gore would eventually sit there.

As fate would have it, the night of this big dinner was the first night of work for our steward Theresa—a real trial by fire! Her first official act was to pour the wine for the evening meal. As she was pouring Penn's wine, Nicholson made a point in the discussion (which seemed like a line he might use in *As Good As It Gets*) and asked Theresa with a sly glance, "Don't you agree?" Though cool-headed every night since, Theresa was so nervous about doing a good job that first night that the only response she could utter was, "Ahhh. Yeah". She confessed to me later that she had no idea what the discussion had been about, nor to what she'd just agreed with Jack Nicholson. Given the actor's reputation, that could have been a delicate predicament indeed!

Nicholson was charming and friendly. He shared many jokes and funny experiences with the Governor. The sun-baked actor was especially chilled and intrigued by the snowy, cold weather we were having – including the snowstorm ongoing as he spoke – and teased the Venturas about it. In all, he was a delight to host. Our only disappointment was that Nicholson didn't drink that night. We'd all heard about his love for liquor and had stocked the Residence pantry with his favorites. The actor must have had a change of palate before he arrived, however, as he politely refused alcohol all evening.

Penn certainly did not reflect his bad boy image. The younger actor was quiet and somewhat reserved and spent a great deal of time talking with Tyrel Ventura, who was interested in being in the movie industry. (In time, Tyrel assisted Penn on a couple of movie projects, including *The Pledge*. Tyrel later moved to California for several months to work on another movie with Penn, and the Penn family also returned a couple years later for the Governor's 50th birthday party.)

The two actors joined the supporting actor-turned-Governor in talking about the movie business for much of the night, swapping stories from the set, and talking about how much time is spent sitting around waiting for a shot to be ready. The Governor shared the story of the practical joke he pulled on his friend, and then coworker, Arnold Schwarzenegger when the two were filming *Predator* in Mexico. It was a story the Governor would also relate in his 1999 book *I Ain't Got Time to Bleed*, named for his famous line in that movie.

His guests smiled and then laughed out loud as the Governor described how he got the best of Arnold when the star bodybuilder let Ventura use his on-set weight room. Ventura would set the alarm early enough to ensure that he beat Schwarzenegger to the weights. He'd then drench himself with water and be sitting there working out when the action hero walked in. His machismo piqued, Schwarzenegger would come to the gym earlier the next day; again Ventura would be there first, looking as if he'd been working out for hours. Eventually, the two were getting up before 4 a.m. to try and beat each other to the workout. Ventura eventually confessed so they could get some sleep, and a lasting friendship was formed from the practical joke.

Between stories, the Governor spent much of the evening doing a hard sell on Minnesota as a movie location. He also joked with his guests several times about the benefits of being Governor, of having people to wait on you, saying it's fun to say 'jump' and have people ask how high.

Governor Ventura wasn't the only diner with wait staff that evening. Penn also brought his body man with him, a personal attendant who went everywhere with the actor. This evening, the attendant appeared to already have had too much to drink, and he was the one who needed attending.

His antics and quirks certainly added to the evening's amusement. He was quite fidgety all evening and was constantly getting up and exploring various rooms. He put firewood in the fireplaces, even though they were already full. He talked loudly throughout the evening, often telling personal stories about Penn and relaying how he would clean up the actor when he had overindulged himself and become sick. Vomit is not exactly formal dinner conversation, even by the Governor's more casual standards.

The attendant also wandered back into the kitchen, which was off limits to guests. I had the challenge of getting him back to the dining room because we did not want him to fall and hurt himself. Fortunately, he teetered to safety at every turn, and the staff's first attempt to entertain celebrities from Hollywood ended as a great success. Both Terry and the Governor thanked staff for a super job.

CHEERS!

The Venturas asked us to put on another Hollywood dinner just a few months later when Woody Harrelson and Steve Guttenberg joined the Governor's table Sept. 14, 1999. They were in the Twin Cities performing a play at a local theatre.

The evening came as close to a disaster as any we hosted at the Residence, though in the end only the staff knew anything about it. Around 4 p.m. that day, just two hours before guests were to arrive, fire broke out above the dining room windows.

Fire at the mansion, which had no sprinkler system and much to lose, was a constant worry for me–so much so that I even had a nightmare about it just a month before. We staff and security were especially concerned because the Venturas' son

Tyrel loved to light candles but often forgot to put them out.

The fire I had long feared broke out when a blowtorch being used to install a new slate roof got too close to some of roof insulation. The second and third floors were filled with smoke, and six St. Paul Fire Department fire trucks surrounded the mansion within minutes. The fire was quickly extinguished and, thankfully, the smoke smell did not make it to the first floor.

Miraculously, and with a bit more hustle than the usual pre-event bustle, we were able to carry on with dinner plans with no one the wiser. Our chefs prepared a Minnesota meal of walleye and wild rice enjoyed by all.

Harrelson and Guttenberg were both down-to-earth guests. Harrelson even wandered back into the kitchen to help mix drinks. The staff quickly discovered that the actor not only played a bartender on television, he knew what he was doing behind the bar. He whipped up shots of tequila, preferably Porfidio. He even invited our steward, Theresa, to join them in a round, which she declined since she was on duty until the Governor said it would be okay to join the group in a shot. When the tequila ran dry, the actor asked for cognac and the festivities continued.

The whole time he was bartending, the *Cheers* star kept staff and the Governor laughing with stories about his TV days. The dinner was filled with good-natured ribbing as the Governor kidded Harrelson about being a vegetarian. To get even, Harrelson later sent a half side of beef to the Residence as a gift to the Governor.

It was a fun evening that went late into the night. Harrelson, known for his long-running role in *Cheers*, ended the evening with a toast by saying simply, "Cheers!" It was a good thing he made the toast when he did as we were out of liquor.

HOT SHOTS

Actors weren't the only stars welcomed to the Governor's Residence. Athletes often visited as well, including popular NBA player Kevin "KG" Garnet, then an all-star forward on the Minnesota Timberwolves professional basketball team.

On August 10, 2000, KG and Jimmy Jam, a local record producer whose clients include Janet Jackson, had come to the mansion to record an NBA video with the Governor. After the work was finished, it was time to play. Garnet was ready to shoot some hoops with the Governor. It was KG and Jimmy Jam against the Governor and a controversial friend of Tyrel's, Stewart Peters (but more on him later). The Governor did fairly well on the court, but he was certainly outplayed. KG blocked almost all of his shots, so the Governor had to shoot from far outside. Needless to say, Garnet's team won.

Many photos were taken that day, including one of me standing alongside Garnet. I came up to KG's belt buckle, and he kept telling me, "White boys can't jump." After the scrimmage, the men decided to stay for an impromptu dinner. I remember that our chef was waiting to serve the meal so he could go home when I had to come in and tell him—with no comments, inquiries or apologies from the Governor—that instead of the First Family, we had a few extra guests with big appetites. The chef somehow stretched a roast to fill everyone's appetite. The food and festivities must have been to KG's liking because he returned again for the Governor's 50th birthday party the following year. Since I am a real fan of KG, I must admit that this was one of my most enjoyable times at the Residence.

A highlight for the Governor was the day that *Survivor* TV show contestant Rudy Boesch accepted the Governor's invitation for appetizers and drinks at the Residence and dinner out on the town. The Governor really wanted to meet Boesch, a fellow veteran and tough talker. The two talked about agents and fame but spent much of the evening reminiscing about their own military adventures, laughing together about the trials of boot camp and training. I never heard either man relate combat stories, but the Governor entertained his guest with stories from his Navy SEAL training, such as how his instructor ripped the skin right off of his blistered hands and how it felt to jump out of an airplane, both stories he told a lot at the mansion and to the public.

Photo shoots, tapings and interviews were commonplace around the Residence. August 4, 2000, was no different as the Governor and his bulldog, Franklin, posed for *Minnesota Monthly* magazine. Waiting in the wings was an even more notable interviewer, Maria Shriver, host of NBC's *Dateline* and wife of Jesse Ventura's friend Arnold Schwarzenegger, with whom the Governor stared in *Predator*.

The Governor explains in his autobiography, *I Ain't Got Time to Bleed*, that he first met Schwarzenegger when the body builder came up to the then World Wrestling Federation announcer to comment on how much he liked The Body's choice of tie-dyed tuxedo. They were more formally introduced on the set of *Predator*, where they became fast friends, especially when Schwarzenegger opened his gym to anyone who wanted to use it—a place where the two weight lifters were soon sharing sweat and practical jokes.

It was Schwarzenegger, the Governor once told me, who introduced him to smoking cigars. The Governor loved to relax with a cigar at night, a habit his actor friend also enjoys.

I had already tasted a bit of that friendship the night the Governor won approval of his first budget in 1999. I went up to the family quarters to congratulate the Governor, and Terry invited me to join them for a glass of champagne. The Governor then offered me a cigar from a box that his good friend Arnold had given him. Though I don't smoke, it was a fine memento from a nice evening with the Venturas.

When Shriver, traveled to Minnesota for the *Dateline* interview, she caught up with the Governor and First Lady during an impromptu salad lunch in the drawing room before filming at the Residence throughout the afternoon.

Shriver was prettier in person than she is on TV, though still quite thin. She was gracious and a pleasure to meet and was kind enough to honor my request for a photo with Terry and me. It was a great shot and appeared in several publications.

The day itself was somewhat helter-skelter because of the film crews running about and some last-minute scheduling changes. Schwarzenegger, who spent the day at the Mall of America with his children in anticipation of the premier of the movie *Jingle All the Way*, was supposed to come to the Residence as well. We were continually preparing for his arrival and then canceling his appearance as the Venturas received update cell phone calls from the actor. In the end, the old friends met up elsewhere that day after Schwarzenegger had had his fill of the mall.

Staff found themselves dealing more than usual with the day's scheduling because the First Lady's press secretary, Erica Carter, had quit that week. Residence staff found ourselves filling in the scheduling gaps on top of keeping up with serving all the guests in the overstuffed mansion.

To add the final layer of frosting to the chaos cake schedulers had baked up for that day, fire alarms went off in the middle of the Governor's interview with Shriver. One of the housekeepers, in desperate need of a 9-volt battery to finish her chores ahead of a film crew, grabbed a battery out of a smoke detector, setting off the siren. There was a moment of wide-eyed nervousness on everyone's part until we could give the Governor the all clear and go back to chaos as usual.

PROTOCOL PRIMERS

Preparing for high-profile visitors always required a bit of extra preparation, but most especially when the Governor hosted political dignitaries from America ... and abroad. They demanded more protocol, and that demanded more detailed research.

For example, in May 2001, the Dalai Lama requested a meeting with the Governor during the Tibetan spiritual leader's visit to speak at the University of Minnesota. The location of the meeting changed several times due to concerns about protests. The Dalai Lama is considered a head of state and was afforded Secret Service protection throughout his visit. Initially, the event was to be a breakfast meeting at the Residence but the meeting was ultimately conducted at the Governor's capitol office.

Though the ball did not land in our court, our staff did a great deal of research preparing for the Dalai Lama's visit. We wanted to make sure protocol was followed regarding proper foods, acceptable greetings, and appropriate seating arrangements. As I did with other foreign and national dignitaries, I consulted with the Minnesota Trade Department, U.S. State Department and the White House to be certain of all details.

We needed to know, for example, if the Dalai Lama could eat meat and if it was proper to shake the Dalai Lama's hand. The answer? Yes, to both.

When the meeting was switched to the Capitol, I was asked to be there to assist the First Lady. I had the opportunity to meet the Dalai Lama and shake hands. He conveys a genuine spirit of humility and concern for his people. When the two leaders started talking, I had high hopes that the Governor would ask the spiritual leader something about how Minnesotans might help him achieve world peace. Instead, I groaned when I heard that he asked this quiet, noble man if he'd ever seen the movie *Caddyshack*. At least the Dalai Lama seemed amused, if not impressed. (I can only imagine Cuban leader Fidel Castro's expression when the Governor later surprised him with an equally inappropriate comment, asking the dictator if he really did have a hand in the President Kennedy's assassination.)

Protocol was always critical when foreign dignitaries were visiting. Small things such as titles, introductions, seating arrangements and speaking schedules could create big misunderstandings. For example, when the French Ambassador to America came to visit, he wanted to speak before the Governor, but Governor Ventura won out and spoke first.

With an off-the-cuff character like Jesse Ventura in the Governor's seat, we were always worried that he would say or do something unexpected that might make Minnesota the epicenter of an international incident. However, Governor Ventura proved adept at meeting, greeting and entertaining dignitaries. When confronted with protocol-sensitive situations, we gave him the appropriate lines and parts to play, and he played them well.

When the Japanese Ambassador was in town in June 2001 and stopped at the Residence for dinner, we had a protocol discussion and even a rehearsal with staff and the Governor to prepare. In addition to bowing protocol, we made a special note to the Governor as to how Japanese business cards should be handled. In Japan, giving someone a business card is like giving them a gift. The recipient is to take it in both hands and read it before putting it in a wallet.

The Governor handled the meeting beautifully. There were a few unexpected, but welcome, protocol hurdles to leap, however, when Former Ambassador to Japan and Former Speaker of the U.S. House of Representatives Tom Foley suddenly arrived at the front door.

When he walked in, there was a moment of hesitation on the part of staff because we had not had time to research the protocol issues, such as whom should be introduced first, Foley or Former Vice President Mondale, who was also in attendance.

Furthermore, we had to quickly decide how to introduce Foley. We opted for standard protocol and introduced him using his most recent title. He was introduced as Ambassador Tom Foley and was a great addition to the event. Foley's height and white hair endeared him to the Japanese people as a man of wisdom and honor. He was given great respect while living in their country, and their respect showed when he visited with them at the Residence. He was gracious and reminisced with guests regarding many of his experiences in government, and he happily consented to a group photo with the staff.

'DANCING' WITH DIGNITARIES

As far as I am aware, the Governor made only one noticeable, but ultimately minor, breach of protocol with his national and international guests.

It was June 7, 1999, the day that real royalty met Minnesota's King of the Ring.

The Crown Prince of Norway, Haakon Magnuf, was an invited lunch guest, and it was a very special day for the Governor and staff. Minnesota has a strong bond with Norway because of trade opportunities as well as the ethnic family ties of so many Minnesotans.

This was our first big media event, and many reporters camped out front to capture the arrival and departure of the Prince. Governor Ventura and the Prince were to speak to the media after lunch.

The Prince was a charming, handsome bachelor and was warm and gracious with the 35 lunch guests, including Lt. Governor Mae Schunk, senior staff members, Minneapolis Mayor Sharon Sales-Belton, St. Paul Mayor Norm Coleman and several Minnesota corporation CEOs. A three-course Minnesota menu with duck as the entrée was served in the solarium. Everything went according to schedule until the Governor and the Crown Prince exchanged gifts.

It is the custom to exchange gifts with a visiting dignitary. I was personally responsible for this aspect of the event, making sure the gift was ready to hand to the Governor. He and I had spoken earlier about the protocol of gift giving. I explained to the Governor that it is improper to give a gift directly to royalty. A close aide would step forward, accept and unwrap the gift for the Prince. This is done as a safety precaution.

The Prince first presented the Governor with a beautiful Norwegian pewter dish with the Prince's monogram inscribed on the top. In his enthusiasm and excitement, the Governor forgot protocol, handed his gift to the prince and insisted he open the box himself. Being gracious, the Prince opened the gift while aides watched closely. The Prince seemed to genuinely appreciate the gift of a beautifully carved, wooden loon and graciously overlooked the Governor's breach in protocol.

In all, the evening had been a royal success, as were all of the dignitary events we hosted at the Residence, beginning with the first on Jan. 28, 1999, my birthday. We welcomed a bit of American political royalty when Anna Eleanor Roosevelt, granddaughter of the famous U.S. First Lady came to visit. Ms. Roosevelt stopped in to attend a 60th anniversary event for the March of Dimes. It was the first official event I helped organize for the Governor. More than 150 people attended and enjoyed the reception, though we were in the middle of a Minnesota snowstorm and not yet up to full staff.

Ms. Roosevelt was the guest speaker, and it was my privilege to meet her. She was dignified and gracious. She spoke of the value of the program her grandfather began 60 years earlier as a result of his own disabling disease. This subject was near and dear to me because of the lifelong disabilities my younger sister suffered from polio.

The Governor was invited to speak at the reception, but he was not scheduled to attend due to another engagement. To everyone's surprise, the Governor did stop in for a few minutes to address the gathering and meet the guest of honor. The Governor spoke for five minutes. He was lively and entertaining. He commented about the great opportunity of living in the Governor's Residence and having a staff that waited on his every need. He invited the guests to make themselves at home but chided them not to steal anything.

The Governor's appearance certainly made the day even more enjoyable. Whenever the Governor wanted to, he could always engage a crowd. He was good with remembering names and people, especially when they were in some way important to him or to others.

The Governor is a talented speaker, even—and maybe especially even—off the cuff. He could be funny, tell stories, take jabs at the audience or be commandingly serious. He especially loved to tell a story that put him in the limelight. For example, after he met President Bush, the Governor's stories revolved around that meeting and around how the President had asked to take a picture with him and wanted him at the presidential table.

Often times, his humor was a play on things delivered with sort of a raised eyebrow approach, such as "I'm going to have the Rolling Stones play for my second inaugural." He'd often joke about that, and the band just might have done it too, especially after the Governor decreed in 1999 that February 15 would be Rolling Stones Day (his first proclamation as Governor).

What made Anna Eleanor Roosevelt's visit special beyond the Governor's charm that day was the fact that her grandmother, Eleanor Roosevelt, visited the mansion during the 1940s while she was First Lady of the United States. She was a friend of the Irvine family and, while visiting the Twin Cities, made a stop at the Summit Avenue home. The Irvine's youngest daughter, Olivia Dodge, remembers how the First Lady agreed to let Olivia take her picture in the lower level family room, where the Irvines displayed a number of President Roosevelt mementos. Olivia was so excited about taking the First Lady's photo that she forgot there was no bulb in the camera. Mrs. Roosevelt graciously informed Olivia she needed a bulb and then waited patiently while Olivia ran upstairs to find one. Olivia was impressed with Mrs. Roosevelt's grace, a characteristic obviously passed down to her granddaughter.

Another legendary political figure, former Minnesota Senator and U.S. Presidential Candidate Eugene McCarthy, visited the Residence for dinner in October 2001. It was truly interesting to meet and speak with the legend of Minnesota politics, who served the state in the U.S. Congress from 1959 to 1971.

Now an elderly man, Senator McCarthy was hard of hearing, and even the booming Governor had to repeat himself often. However, the Governor was unusually patient, engaging and animated with the Senator throughout the evening. He seemed entranced by everything the Senator had to say, in part, I believe, because the Governor recognized that he was dining with a fellow political maverick. McCarthy had attracted young voters to his 1968 presidential campaign, primarily because of his opposition to the Vietnam War. The Governor seemed to identify with Senator McCarthy's combative style and stand-alone type politics.

PRESIDENTIAL PROTOCOL

The Minnesota Governor's mansion, and Irvine residence, has long played host to political dignitaries, including some of the most well known in the world, from President and Mrs. Gorbachev of the former Soviet Union to Princess Margaret and Lord Snowdon of England.

Of the high-profile political guests Governor Ventura would welcome, none required more preparation simply because of his presence than then U.S. Vice President Al Gore. He and his wife Mary Tipper Gore stayed overnight at the Residence as guests of the Venturas June 21, 2000, during Gore's presidential campaign. The Governor and First Lady had visited the Gores at the Vice President's home in Washington, D.C., on a previous trip and had extended an offer for the Gores to visit them in Minnesota.

Preparing for the Gores' visit was like producing a play. There were weeks of preparation for one night's performance. Like any high-level visit, plans and details—including both the date and venue for the visit—changed many times. At several points, the visit was even canceled. In the end, everything went like clockwork.

The Secret Service advanced the visit several days ahead. I met with them on several occasions, walking through the Residence. We viewed the guest room where the Gores would stay, established the location of the Secret Service command post (located in the carriage house) and, most importantly, worked out security issues. The Secret Service swept the Residence with trained dogs and also went through neighbors' houses with dogs to search for any weapons or other suspicious items.

Twelve additional phone lines were installed. Some were fax lines, and some were secured lines that enabled the Vice President to be in touch with the President if needed. This detailed routine is followed for every presidential or vice presidential visit, regardless of where they travel. The average citizen cannot imagine the level of advance work involved whenever the President or Vice President travel. It is, of course, Secret Service protocol.

The Venturas kept their pink bedroom but gave up their second-floor family room, thus giving the Vice President and Mrs. Gore a mini suite, which included the newly remodeled burgundy and gold guest bedroom, sitting room, bath and enclosed porch. Sandy and Jean did an excellent job helping me prepare the room with snacks, beverages and a gift basket of Minnesota treats filled with items from wild rice to local wines.

Everyone was working twice as hard and twice as fast to make the Residence presidential. Our chefs had gone into an extra high gear as they prepared the food not only for the VIPs but for the Secret Service working out of the carriage house. They went so far as to bake gourmet cookies and hand frost them. Sylvia, the staff member in charge of feeding the carriage house contingent, delivered the cookies to the Secret Service.

We teased Sylvia about trusting her with the special cookies since a few weeks earlier she had accidentally served a platter of event-bound cookies to a tour group. (Sylvia had immediately confessed to the crime and helped the day's cookie baker, Theresa, whip up a new batch in time for the event.)

The Secret Service guys loved the tray of cookies Sylvia brought them. One agent in particular was *inhaling* them. Sylvia called the chef to ask him to make more cookies. It was the wrong request to make of a man cooking on unusually thin frosting. The chef couldn't understand how a whole tray of cookies disappeared so quickly and stormed out of the kitchen and over to the carriage house to confront Sylvia, a known cookie thief (from the previous incident). He looked around, saw the empty tray, pointed at Sylvia and yelled, 'Why did you eat all my cookies!

Sylvia's quick wit combined with an unusually tried and tired temper. In the split second it took for the chef to point his finger, Sylvia whapped the chef upside the head and shouted: "Don't you ever come up here in front of people and accuse me of eating your cookies! I know it looks like I could eat a tray of cookies, but I didn't! It was that guy!" She pointed at the federal agent with frosting-coated lips and his hand in the cookie jar.

The chef took one look at the fire in Sylvia's eyes and retreated so fast from the carriage house that his feet didn't even touch the stairs. The dumbfounded agents just stared slack jawed at the sweet housemother who'd gone feral before their eyes. Perhaps out of concern for his own safety—or desire to get more cookies—one agent tried to break the ice by telling Sylvia that the Secret Service might have a job for her. Sylvia shot back, "Do you really want to put a gun in my hand right now?" Everyone laughed, but the Secret Service never made the offer again. And, Sylvia had the tray of cookies she'd requested in world record frosting time.

The tense anticipation of preparing for the vice presidential visit was only exceeded by the Gores' arrival. Tipper Gore arrived in town first on a separate airplane. She had been campaigning in a different city. She went to the Ventura ranch in Maple Grove to meet with Terry. Theresa went to the ranch to serve refreshments for their meeting because Terry was busy getting Jade ready for a riding competition, which took place that evening at the Minnesota State Fair grounds.

Vice President Gore traveled directly to the Residence. We were all at the windows watching for him like little children waiting for Christmas. The Secret Service did not allow any staff to greet him outside. The Governor even waited inside the solarium as a security procedure. When the motorcade pulled into the gates, one would have thought a small army had descended upon the Residence as approximately 20 vehicles came speeding inside.

The Vice President travels with a host of personal assistants and attendants. His entourage included one or two personal stewards, secretaries, military personnel, a doctor, an ambulance driver and even a fire fighter. The group is equipped for any emergency. I worked closely with his steward, verifying the menu for the evening meal, the dress attire and numerous other details.

Upon arrival, Vice President Gore was whisked inside. Al Gore is taller in person than he appears on television. He was tan and in shape and exceptionally engaging and friendly. Vice President Gore greeted each staff member lined up to meet him. After he and the Governor shook hands, the staff started to leave, but the Vice President insisted, "No, get back here. We're going to have a picture." His photographer took our picture, with Cassandra and Sylvia standing on either side of the vice president—and the Governor down on the end of the lineup—and later sent each of us a copy.

Mrs. Gore arrived from the ranch shortly after the Vice President and they kissed, though not quite as passionately as at the Democratic Convention. My immediate impression of Mrs. Gore was that she was pretty, much prettier in person than on TV. Her dress was modest, even conservative, as was her makeup. She wore no strong perfume and seemed extremely down to earth and instantly conveyed genuine warmth to those who met her. She did not, even from the first moment, seem to be the typical Washington, D.C., type.

The Governor gave the Gores a tour of the Residence and its gardens. They seemed impressed with the beauty of it all. The Governor and First Lady enjoyed showing off the colorful, lush gardens to their guests, and the Governor often quipped, as he did to the Gores, that he had done all the work himself.

Sylvia, the unofficial staff photographer, tagged along on the tour and took pictures of her own for staff scrapbooks. She took lots of photos during the Gores' visit, but we often joke that all we have to show for all the photos Sylvia took is one scrapbook of feet and another of blurry faces.

In late afternoon, Governor Ventura and the Gores departed to meet the First Lady at the fairgrounds. They all watched Jade's riding competition. Though she usually does quite well, Jade had fallen and cut her leg a few days before and didn't place in the event. When they returned to the Residence, Mr. and Mrs. Gore listened to Jade play the piano for them before sitting down for a late dinner with the Venturas. I was impressed that the Gores were so eager for the Venturas to continue with their family plans instead of expecting special arrangements or enter-tainment. It was clear by their actions, and their genuine inter-est in supporting Jade's activities that night, that family and family time are something the Gores value.

Dinner was served around 10 p.m., and the chef had pre-pared a true Minnesota meal of walleye and wild rice. Terry and Mrs. Gore retired early, but the Governor and Vice President sat out on the terrace until around 1 a.m., enjoying drinks and cigars. I planned to sleep that evening in my office, but never made it. Security was on duty around the clock, so I stayed up to tend to their needs. We provided food and beverage throughout the night for everyone who needed to be awake.

The Governor and Vice President left together early the next morning to appear at a local school. They were out the door by 6 a.m., but Mrs. Gore did not leave until around 10 a.m. After the steward served her breakfast in her room, she came downstairs. As her staff prepared final details for her departure, I had about 15 minutes to visit with her. She was extremely personable. We talked mainly about their children. I inquired about their son, who had been in a serious accident. Since I had researched her educational background and knew she had a master's degree in psychology, we also chatted about children and family values. Mrs. Gore was reflective. She talked about the importance of being able to spend time with children and the challenge they had because they were always on the road, especially during the campaign. Their son's accident reminded them how important family time could be. It was obvious that Mrs. Gore is a devoted mother.

When she was ready to leave, Mrs. Gore told me that she and the Vice President thoroughly enjoyed their visit. She related how peaceful and calm the time had been. It was what they needed in the midst of a hectic campaign schedule. She also stated that it was obvious the staff loved the Venturas and cared a great deal about the Residence. She gave me a hug, and I walked her to the car.

As we crossed under the portico, Mrs. Gore invited me to visit the Vice President's home in Washington, D.C. In all seriousness, she said to have my people contact her people. My wife and I have laughed about that comment many times since I have no people.

I was also presented with a beautiful set of Vice Presidential cuff links, given to me by Mr. Gore's steward before he left for the airport. He said the Gores truly enjoyed their visit and wanted to give the cuff links as a token of their appreciation. The Secret Service also awarded the staff members with lapel pins, saying this was one of the best stays they had enjoyed anywhere—cookies and all!

The steward then invited the staff to the airport to tour Air Force Two. We took him up on the offer. It was exciting to see inside where few people get to go. The staff waited for the Vice President to arrive back at Air Force Two so they could say good-bye.

When I arrived back at the Residence, so did one of Tipper's staffers. It seemed Mrs. Gore had forgotten a $2 candle someone had given her. She remembered the omission and rushed someone back to get it. Mrs. Gore was just that apple pie.

Thus ended a whirlwind visit. I personally left for home that night feeling uplifted as an American. I learned that day how down to earth a Vice President and his wife could be, and I went home with a deep and lasting respect for the Gores as parents and as a couple.

THEN, THERE'S THE DOG

Though always memorable, not all of the Venturas' houseguests earned such respect.

The most vexing mansion guest was the smallest, the Venturas' pet bulldog, Franklin, a stout little package that caused the biggest protocol problems the Governor encountered. Even the Governor's most notable guests met, and will never forget, Minnesota's First Dog. Just ask former U.S. Vice President Walter Mondale.

Vice President Mondale met Franklin Feb. 4, 1999, when Governor Ventura hosted a business lunch for the Rand Corporation. This lunch was no different than any other of the dozens of luncheons that the Governor hosted, except for the friendship that Franklin struck up with Mr. Mondale.

Franklin loved attention and he especially wanted some this day. To get noticed, the bulldog would often attach himself to someone's leg, with all four of his legs wrapped around theirs. Once attached, he did not want to let go.

Naturally, of all the legs in the room, Franklin chose to start humping the former Vice President's. This was an embarrassing moment for Mr. Mondale, the Governor and the staff, for everyone except Franklin. After several commands, Franklin finally let go, and he was banished to the security office. The staff helped clean the slobber off Mr. Mondale's pants, and the lunch proceeded without any other incidents with the exception of a few stifled snickers. Thankfully, the Vice President was a good sport and returned as a guest several times despite this passionate moment. His buddy Franklin, however, was never invited for an encore.

I also experienced many encounters with Franklin. One day, while I waited for the First Lady under a balcony, Franklin came to the landing and stuck his head in between the railings. He often spewed slobber, and this occasion was no different. Suddenly, a big blob of slobber dropped from his mouth and landed squarely on top of my head. This incident did not exactly endear Franklin to me.

Many times Franklin was a pest. One morning, the staff could not find the dog. We called for him and looked everywhere. I was loading my car with supplies to take to the Capitol when I noticed Franklin had crawled up on the back seat and snuggled on top of my best suit jacket.

Needless to say, I did relish the day that the Governor's Residence got even with its most trying guest. Franklin was relaxing in the backyard when the sprinkler system started automatically. The sprinklers came up out of the ground, one exactly where Franklin was lying, jabbing him in his belly. It startled him and he attacked the sprinkler, chewing it into pieces.

Franklin looks slow going, but when he wanted to move, he could. He loved to chase fish around the cement pond and, if he spotted a squirrel, that dog could move at top speed. He spotted a lot of squirrels. The squirrels seemed to enjoy tormenting Franklin.

Top speed was not Franklin's usual posture, however. Most days he could be found sprawled out on the floor, in the yard, in my car. During a black-tie event, Franklin sprawled in the middle of the foyer, making himself at home even though he was not wearing a black tie. Theresa was carrying a tray of filled champagne glasses. As she stepped backward to allow a guest to pass by, she fell over Franklin. Thankfully, she was not hurt and, once again, Franklin was banished to the security office.

Franklin spent a lot of time in the security office. In fact, when the First Family was out of the town, it was security who drew the short straw on taking care of the First Canine, including wrapping his daily medicine in cheese (perhaps not the best choice for a dog with flatulence problems) and getting the stubborn bulldog to swallow.

Most memorable was Franklin's performance at another formal event, The 1006 Society Residence fund-raising fashion show, an annual favorite. The show featured seasonal fashions from such stores as Macy's and Neiman Marcus modeled by professional models, members of the 1006 Society, the First Lady, her mother Sharon Larson and the Venturas' daughter Jade. Three hundred and fifty guests gathered in a huge tent in the backyard for the 1999 show. As usual, Franklin was working the crowd. Though the Governor attended for a while, it was the First Dog who proved the day's showstopper.

Observing the models going up the steps to the stage and walking to each corner, Franklin decided he too could walk the runway, despite his lack of appropriate seasonal attire. At the most opportune moment, Franklin bounded up on stage and did exactly what each model did. Needless to say, he stole the show. Franklin's photo, not the First Lady's, made the front page the next day.

Perhaps the First Dog's only official contribution was to serve as a secret weapon (and, I suspected, an occasionally convenient cover) for the Governor, proving perhaps that dogs cannot only look like their owners but sound like them as well.

Franklin, let's just say, has a constant gaseous condition. Once, when a few legislative leaders were at the Residence debating the budget bill, the Governor allowed the members to wait in the library. Franklin wandered into the room. Lacking in social graces and feeling right at home, Franklin immediately changed the air quality inside the room. By the time the meeting convened, the legislators were ready to agree to anything. Perhaps Franklin should have been invited more often to these meetings.

| CHAPTER 3 |

JESSE: THE 'FUN RAISER'

Despite the occasional canine interruptions, life at the Residence ran like clockwork, revolving around the Governor's and First Lady's schedules.

I usually arrived at the mansion between 7 and 8 a.m. so I'd be there when the Governor was ready to leave, in case I needed to remind him of something or discuss a mansion matter with him. Staff arrived on a somewhat staggered schedule. For example, we had one chef from morning through lunch and another for lunch through dinner. Our steward was on duty in the kitchen from 11 a.m. through dinner and housekeepers were staggered based on the day's needs.

Office staff met in the morning to go over the day's business. On a rare day that we didn't have an event, we prepared for the next one, researching protocol and deciding on decorations, menu, and staffing. In addition, I spent a great deal of time working on restoring and maintaining the physical property itself. As the mansion staff representative, I served on the 1006 Society and Governor's Residence Council boards, which met monthly to plan and discuss fund-raising and upkeep of the mansion.

Nearly every day we had a luncheon to set, serve and clean up. We also had many breakfasts and dinners at the Residence each week. During evening events, staff stayed through the meal and I would post myself in the room where the meal was being served to ensure we could meet anyone's needs. Staff would also sample the meal ahead of time so we could describe the ingredients and taste to guests. There were occasions when Terry would invite me to eat with them. While I appreciated the thought, I'd always declined because I didn't think it proper protocol for staff to be eating with the guests.

Staff would eat afterwards in the kitchen and stay to clean up. No staff left the mansion until the Residence was clean and back to working order. This often meant late nights. When he was on a roll, the Governor was known to entertain late into the evening. There were certainly times when I slept in my own office after an event, so I could wake early to prepare for a breakfast meeting and another full day.

Thrown into the day's mix were a variety of planned and spontaneous media interviews. The local and national media were a constant presence during the Ventura era, and many interviews were scheduled at the Residence. Hosting interviews that coincided with live broadcasts could be especially taxing and often consumed a great deal of time, such as predawn arrivals of camera crews. For example, if the Governor was going to be on one of the early morning shows, I was at the Residence by 4 a.m. to work with the crew.

The longest day I remember was on Feb. 16, 1999, when the Governor was interviewed live on the *Today Show* at 6 a.m. I arrived at 4 a.m. to let the crew inside, worked through the day and stayed late that evening because the Governor was scheduled for the *Tom Snyder Show* at midnight. I clocked in over 21 hours that day and enjoyed every minute of it.

Beyond this hectic schedule, the staff quickly learned to be prepared for pop-up events. Every so often, the Governor would move a meeting from the Capitol to the Residence, a surprise event that happened more and more towards the end of his term when he felt less comfortable at the Capitol. It also happened in cases where guests might need a more discreet, less public setting. For example, many budget meetings, such as those with the president of the university, were held at the mansion, as was a meeting with the president of Northwest Airlines. Other times, the Venturas, like other First Families, would have personal guests and friends stay the night at the mansion, requiring meal, snack and cleaning service beyond the First Family's regular needs.

The constantly changing schedule produced so many hectic days that the staff started calling me "the mouse" or "mouse-man" because, they told me, they could always hear me scurrying around the mansion.

It seemed that I was always running to do a number of things at the same time. One day, my speed cost me. I was carrying a 16th Century chair from upstairs to the main level via the back stairway. Because the steps are narrow, I slipped and fell down the stairs. As I tumbled, my concern was to save the chair, which landed without a scratch on top of me. My fast feet were not so lucky, however. My ankle was sprained and swelled up so much that I had to go to the doctor and slow my scampering for a few weeks.

Though such days could certainly try one's stamina, we loved serving the Venturas and the People's House. I always left the Residence after a long night's event with a smile, knowing we'd done well and that the Venturas and the state looked good to the guests we hosted.

TOURS OF DUTY

When we weren't preparing, serving and cleaning, mansion office staff and myself were often hosting public events and leading tours of our stately home.

It was Terry Ventura's desire to ensure the Residence lived up to its image as The People's House. As past Governors had, the Venturas opened the doors to public tours, and Terry specifically asked that we make the Residence more available to public groups. Under new procedures outlined by Terry and myself, many civic, nonprofit, educational and community groups were able to reserve the Residence for meetings. By billing out the mansion's direct costs, such groups were able to use the facility with little, if any, expense to the state.

Staff thoroughly enjoyed every opportunity to share this beautiful building with as many people as possible. It is, indeed, the people's home first and a state treasure, placed on both St. Paul Historic Sites Register in 1978 and the National Register of Historic Places in 1974. Guests frequently marveled at how such a splendid mansion could radiate the warmth of a home. That atmosphere was generated by the care and concern of each staff member who had the honor of working in such a special and unique place.

We received many compliments from the groups that met at the Residence, but our greatest compliments came from the 6,000 guests who took the public tours annually. Many of these were held during special events the Residence hosted, including our annual open houses around Halloween and Christmas. The several thousand people who came through the open houses were invited to tour the main levels. As they exited, the children were given caramel apples and bags of candy donated by local candy companies.

Each year the staff elaborately decorated the Residence for both open house events with designs we chose and created to surprise the Venturas and the state. Each year, the First Family expressed their delight in the decorations, and the Governor would often quip to guests how his home "always looked like Christmas."

The decorating took a great deal of time, but the general public thoroughly enjoyed the sights each season. Some years, companies such Department 56, Target and local florists also volunteered time and expense to help decorate the Residence, inside and outside.

Halloween was the staff favorite. We'd all dress up to give tours, and some staff would venture out to the gate on All Hollow's Eve to hand out candy. Staff really got into the spooky décor. We did so much with donated decorations and a lot of creativity that our Halloween decorations were even featured in *Department 56* magazine. Staff transformed the solarium into a graveyard and the family room into a haunted theater complete with ghostly manikins in theater seats intermingled with costumed staff, which would turn in their seat and say "Boo!" One year, Sylvia and Sandy talked Theresa into posing as a headless entrée underneath a silver platter on the dining room table. When the guests left, staff innocently forgot (or so they say) about Theresa and went into other rooms to start cleaning up. We didn't hear Theresa yelling for someone to open up the table and let her out, but she eventually pried herself from the table and crawled out. Then things really got scary!

Speaking of scary, no one at the mansion will soon forget one particular group of nighttime visitors. At the invitation of a local radio show, a group of casually attired Minnesotans appeared at the Residence gates one night to send the Governor a memorable message. At that crack of midnight, they mooned the mansion! I'm not sure if their message got through, *butt* their image will never be forgotten.

For all the thousands of visitors to the Residence, there was only one frightening security incident during the Ventura's administration involving challengers of a Highway 55 road construction project, which was routed through an ancient Indian burial ground. In 1999, six protestors got inside the Residence by joining the Christmas open house tour line. Wanting to get the Governor's attention, they created a loud scene by yelling crude remarks at the Governor who, with the First Lady, was welcoming the public to the Christmas open house. A dozen state police on duty inside the Residence quickly subdued the protesters and led them away.

The Governor was across the room and the First Lady was standing next to me when the ruckus erupted. Instinctively I led Terry into another room. The entire staff was protective of the First Lady and always wanted to make sure she and her children were safe.

On no other day during the Ventura administration did we feel that more strongly than on Sept. 11, 2001. The Venturas were as shocked as every American by the terrorist attacks carried out that day. As political leaders, they were probably more personally affected since concern that national politicians, and even governors, could be targets grew for a time as the day's events unfolded.

I was in the Residence office early that morning and was watching the *Today* show, when it aired the incredible footage of a burning World Trade Center tower. I was staring unbelievably at the screen and saw the second airplane crash into the other tower.

Immediately, I went upstairs and told the Governor the news. He was in disbelief and just stared at me as I stared back in silence for a moment. At first, he thought, as we all did—all wanted to—that it may have been a bizarre plane crash. As the events unfolded and reality hit us between the eyes, the Governor had a not-surprising Navy SEAL reaction, "Let's go get them!"

Security staff reacted strongly as well, and state police immediately secured the Residence and government buildings in case the Capitol, Residence or Governor, might be a target. State police rushed to get Terry from the Maple Grove home and Jade from school and bring them to the Residence. Guests of the Venturas, who had stayed overnight Sept. 10, were locked in at the mansion with every one else that day. The Governor, who went to the Capitol earlier that morning, was soon brought back to the Residence. Vendors or outside workers were ushered out of the mansion immediately. In the meantime, additional state police vehicles were brought into the compound to block gates from unwelcome intruders. For our part, Residence staff scurried to ensure we had adequate food and supplies on hand for a lock down that could last a few days.

The First Lady was in tears when she and Jade arrived at the mansion. Terry reacted more emotionally to the news because of the security response and because the Venturas were concerned about a good friend stationed at the Pentagon. The Governor expressed little emotion outwardly, but tried to comfort his wife and children and convince them they were safe and things would be okay.

I found time to call my family at home and do the same. Though the Venturas and security said we could go home to be with family if we wanted, staff chose to stay. I cannot speak to all of staff's motivations for staying on, but I personally felt that I should stay there to do what I could to help the Venturas and the state in such a tragic time. Other staff and I stayed late into the evening to provide food and snacks to the extra security and the Venturas.

It was a tense and unusually quiet time in the mansion. No one could believe what had just happened, the Governor included, and everyone was trying to decide what to do next.

Like the rest of America, the Governor decided that we should get back to "normal," with some heightened security awareness.

A few weeks later, the Governor and First Lady organized an official memorial for the citizens of Minnesota on the steps of the Capitol. More than 30,000 gathered to hear tributes from civic and religious leaders and music from local artists. Dozens of fire trucks converged on the Capitol mall from around the state to pay respect to their fallen comrades. As the event concluded, the trucks formed a long parade home with lights flashing and sirens soulfully blaring.

FUN & FUND-RAISING

The Residence was a safe haven that day for the First Family, but it was always a comfortable place to be and the First Lady was as enamored with the Residence as anyone who worked or visited there was.

Terry Ventura worked hard to preserve and improve the Residence she enjoyed, and went to substantial efforts to raise money for the mansion's upkeep. A major project that the First Lady wanted to accomplish was to host fund-raising events for the mansion. These funds were to replace furniture, rugs and drapes plus other special projects. During the Ventura term, the Governor and First Lady hosted three formal fund-raising dinners, costing $1,000 per person, for 40 guests each. Set up in the solarium, the elegant dinners created by our French-trained chefs generally cleared at least $25,000 each after expenses.

Proceeds were allocated for major remodeling projects such as new wall coverings in the lower level family and conference rooms. Other projects included replacing some Oriental rugs, reupholstering numerous pieces of antique furniture and repairing lighting fixtures.

At the same time Terry Ventura started the fund-raising dinners, she began hosting public dinners attended by a variety of Minnesotans. Credit should be given to the First Lady for trying to use the Residence to serve the people, even though she did not always have the Governor's support.

I still remember the first public dinner. Since Terry wanted a cross section of guests, we had invited three couples that included a college professor, a dentist, a career counselor, a retired businessman and two college students. Despite a heavy snowstorm, all six guests made it to the Residence on time. No one, it seemed, wanted to miss an opportunity to spend a private evening with the Governor and First Lady.

No one, that is, except the Governor. Early in the day he had expressed to the First Lady, and anyone within earshot, that he did not want to attend the dinner—a sentiment often expressed when it came to attending almost anything at the Residence. He grumbled and complained, but the First Lady finally convinced him to join the table. As the evening progressed, the Governor began to enjoy himself and entertained our guests with stories and memories.

Frequently, as he did that night, the Governor would tell stories about the Residence being haunted. Many believe the house is haunted because Elizabeth, the Irvines' oldest daughter died in the home after she returned there with her children from a failing marriage. Nearly all of the staff, including myself, had occasional experiences with Elizabeth brushing by us in an empty hall, moving things about or slamming doors. Many of us heard her footsteps running on the back service staircase, a nearly monthly event, which security always investigated but could never explain.

Some staff experienced spookier encounters than others. For example, one day Theresa was in the garden picking flowers for a table setting. While she was gone, one of the chefs came into the kitchen. About 15 minutes later, Theresa walked in and the chef said, "Oh, you're back already." Theresa explained that she had not been in the kitchen, and the chef insisted that they had just talked to her there a minute or two before.

Our housekeeper Sandy also swears that Elizabeth redid her work while she was putting away china in the dining room. She had set the china on the sofa as she loaded it into the large buffet. When she finished, Sandy looked back at the sofa to ensure she hadn't forgotten anything and went to the kitchen. A few moments later, I went into the room and found several pieces of china tossed on the sofa. Irritated that they'd been left there, I went to the kitchen to ask Sandy about it. She insisted they'd all been in the buffet when she left!

Another night, while staff was waiting in the nook for the Governor and guests to finish in the dining room, the lights went out but only in the dining room. Theresa went in to see if the Governor was all right and he kidded her, "Are you trying to tell us something? Why did you turn the lights off?" No guest or staff had turned them off, and no circuit breaker had been blown. Theresa crossed the room and flipped the switch back on, but it was moments like these when we could feel the hairs on the back of our necks stand up.

The Governor especially enjoyed telling about an incident

that happened to him one February evening when he and his writer were alone in the Residence. Mysteriously, a cabinet door opened and a tea set fell to the floor in the pantry. Several dishes were broken. There was no plausible explanation for this occurrence. The Governor loved to embellish this story and, of course, the guests enjoyed hearing the spooky account.

Beyond being a good storyteller, Jesse Ventura loved to share his opinion with anyone who asked, or anyone he believed would benefit from it. That first night, one of the college students at the dinner was majoring in public relations. The Governor spent much of the evening lecturing the student about the pitfalls of the local press—how they do not report the news accurately but corrupt it by adding their slanted and biased views.

Though the Governor, once he was there, seemed to enjoy the few public dinners scheduled during those first two years, he eventually said he would not participate any longer. Further public dinners were canceled. Those few citizens who were invited considered it a privilege to dine at the mansion and especially to have the personal time with the Governor and First Lady. It was a great idea while it lasted.

The mansion wasn't the only beneficiary of Terry Ventura's fund-raising efforts. The First Lady has a great love for children, especially for those who have special needs. Shortly after the election, Terry and Jesse Ventura organized a foundation, the Jade Foundation. Named after their daughter, the organization helped fund groups that normally do not receive assistance from the state. The Residence hosted many Jade Foundation press conferences throughout the four years of Governor Ventura's administration, often announcing the dispersion of money raised, such as a donation to a riding club that uses horseback riding as physical therapy for children with special needs.

Numerous times, the First Lady hosted schools for children with special needs, such as Courage Center and the Fraser House, bringing their students to the Residence for lunch and entertainment. On one occasion, when the cast of *Beauty and The Beast* was in town for a performance, they agreed to perform a variety of musical numbers at the Residence for special education students. The children loved the music and the colorful costumes.

In December 2000, nationally celebrated pianist and Minnesota native Lori Line performed a concert in Minneapolis to help raise money for the Jade Foundation. Line was already a good friend and supporter of Terry Ventura's charity work and had attended numerous functions at the Residence in conjunction with events the First Lady hosted. The pianist had also donated a number of her CDs to the Residence to be used for background music.

The Governor even attended the December concert, although the First Lady had confided in me that her husband thought he would not like it. To his amazement, the Governor thoroughly enjoyed the music and Ms. Line's splendid costuming and entertaining style. Lori Line and her husband Tim were later invited to dinner at the Residence and proved to be a warm and gracious couple.

The First Lady also took the opportunity to host social events at the Residence, including the annual afternoon reception for the Dome Club, an organization consisting of spouses and significant others of legislators. This function afforded the First Lady an opportunity to get to know this group in a relaxed setting.

We wanted to include special entertainment and hired a local trio of entertainers, Triple Espresso, to perform a portion of their comedy routine on a small stage on the terrace. The trio rose to the political occasion and ribbed the legislative spouses about the legislators and how politicians were the lucky ones who got to have all the fun. Their act encouraged audience participation, and they kidded with the First Lady about being married to the boss. Terry took the ribbing well, and the guests were highly entertained on this day at the Residence.

Because the University of Minnesota had a good relationship with the Governor's office going back to the Carlson administration, there were many requests to hold events at the Residence, an inquiry we honored when we could. One notable evening in the summer of 1999, the Residence hosted a reception for Dr. Barry Levy, President of the American Public Health Forum, who was in town for a series of lectures. Dr. Levy, a gifted scholar, spoke to the group of more than 100 Residence guests and was engaging and considerate to everyone present. Unfortunately, the Governor had chosen not to attend.

Among the most frequent official guests were Minnesota University President and his wife, Mark and Judy Yudof, who attended a number of events at the Residence during the Ventura years, including a private dinner with the Governor and First Lady. To my knowledge, this dinner was the only time the staff "goofed" with a menu request. I knew the dietary restrictions regarding kosher meats for the Yudofs, but somehow we missed the request for fruit to be served to Mark Yudof as his dessert. Usually denied sugar, Mr. Yudof was more than happy to eat the cake that had been prepared, but his wife interceded and the staff immediately got him the correct dessert.

On Feb. 16, 2000, the Minnesota Governor's Residence was officially dedicated as a World Peace site, the first governor's Residence in the United States to earn this distinction. As a result, a United Nations flag flies atop the Residence flagpole. The First Lady and Lieutenant Governor Mae Schunk spoke on behalf of the Governor, who declined to attend the event due to a scheduling conflict and his desire for the First Lady to have center stage on the subject. World Peace Site officials spoke about the heightened awareness that the Residence would offer by accepting this distinction and how important such sites could be for promoting peace among children. To emphasize this intent, the First Lady invited children from several local schools to sing.

The First Lady did a gubernatorial job as host in her husband's absence, a performance she enacted many times at the Residence since the Governor generally ducked such events. He was more likely, however, to attend political events the Residence hosted.

I was especially pleased, for example, when the Governor showed up to meet my fellow residence managers who were attending the National Governor's Association Residence Managers Conference we were hosting at the Governor's Mansion in 2000.

Our meetings were held in the solarium and lunch was served under a tent on the terrace. One of the most frequent comments was how jealous other residence managers were of my office space; most of them had broom closets. A formal dinner was planned and the Governor stopped by to say a few words, including some kind ones about the job I was doing for him and for the state. I was standing behind the Governor after having introduced him and was pleased when he stated publicly that I was doing a great job. I was especially touched by his comments about how Terry and I had worked together to transform the house into a home while maintaining the dignity on the mansion. The Governor was in good form that evening and agreed to have photos taken with each guest. He also autographed copies of his book, *I Ain't Got Time To Bleed*, and presented one to each guest.

Later that year, the Governor was actually excited to attend a special dinner he and the First Lady hosted for Minnesota's entire Washington, D.C., delegation Dec. 27. The staff prepared an elegant and relaxing evening and, despite political differences, the Governor was engaging with everyone, including U.S. Senator Paul Wellstone. The late senator, a two-term Democrat, and the Governor were often at odds politically. The Governor and Senator had come to cross words often—at least in the press—especially after the Governor said he might run against Wellstone for U.S. Senate and rumors flew that Wellstone might fight Ventura for the Governorship if Ventura ran for reelection. The Senator called the Governor an "I guy," and as a former collegiate wrestler, Wellstone added that the theme of their political contest could be "the real wrestler versus the fake wrestler."

The Capitol staff had, in fact, instructed us to be certain that Senator Wellstone and the Governor were seated at different tables to avoid uneasiness.

That may be been an unnecessary step since both men were quite cordial to each other throughout the evening. And though the Governor was often at odds with Senator Wellstone politically, he did seem to respect the senator's strong determination and fiery spirit for his beliefs. The Governor also appreciated the way the political maverick could rally the young people to vote as he himself had done.

The staff was impressed with Senator Wellstone as well. The Senator suffered with back pain and came into the kitchen midway through the evening to get an aspirin. In spite of obvious discomfort, the Senator visited and joked with the staff for several minutes. He took the time to thank each of us for a fine evening. It was these unplanned moments that made our jobs at the Residence really special and memorable.

When Senator Wellstone was killed in a plane crash two years later, in late October 2002, my first thought was how personable he had been that evening. I was saddened that Minnesota had lost a real statesman and a passionate and gracious man. Senator Wellstone truly understood grassroots politics. After all, he had been the only Residence dinner attendee who called the next day to thank everyone for a great evening. Not even the Governor had taken time to do so.

JUST PLAIN FUN

Serving the Governor, his guests and the state of Minnesota was certainly hard work, but that doesn't mean we didn't find time to play. The jovial group of staffers I oversaw liked to keep me, and each other, on our toes.

The staff often played practical jokes as a means of coping with the pressure of the job. One day, for example, I took a giant stuffed Golden Plump chicken, which had been given to the Governor, and put it in Sylvia's chair when she was out sick. I attached a note that read, 'We see that any featherbrain can do your job!'"

Another time, my joke was unintended. Sylvia, who speaks English and Spanish fluently, came to the rescue of the Governor when the Ambassador to Mexico was visiting and the two were trying to talk about television shows they liked. With such important business to discuss, the Governor was desperate for a translator and called Sylvia over. I wanted to give her a pat on the back and e-mailed our boss, Chief of Staff Steven Bosacker, to praise Sylvia's extra efforts. My praise didn't have the intended effect, however, because of an unfortunate typo. Instead of glowing over how well Sylvia had interpreted for the Governor, I told Steven "Sylvia really did a good job *interrupting* for the Governor." (Like Jesse Ventura needed help interrupting!)

Sylvia got me back in style, however, and more than once. On my 50th birthday, Sylvia and staff littered my office with confetti. Hundreds of tiny "50" symbols were lodged in every drawer, book, plant and file. Everyone knows what a neat freak I am, and it still took me weeks to find them all!

Staff probably got me best, however, when several hid in my coat closet one winter morning. When I opened the door to hang my coat, they screamed and proved to my wife once and for all that I do not have a serious heart condition!

We were all screaming when Mother Nature played her own joke on the Residence and invited a large, gap-toothed rat into the mansion. He came up out of a toilet in the lower level, leaving clumps of hair on the toilet seat. He naturally liked the kitchen best. Knife handles were often found chewed up; and he got into the pantry for his own little snack party more than once. An exterminator came five times but it was the chefs who finally convinced our furry guest to leave.

Something as gross as a rat in the pantry was more than enough ammunition for the queen of staff practical jokers, Sandy. She got a rubber rat and put it in the downstairs bathroom, causing Sylvia to reach a screaming pitch not often heard outside of opera houses. Sandy next put the rat in a pastry bag on the kitchen counter, leaving just a tail hanging out of the edge of the bag for Theresa to find when she came in from the garden. After nearly jumping out of her skin and raising a ruckus so loud that security came running, the agents and Theresa teamed up to get even and put the rat in the microwave. It was Sandy's turn to scream that night when she went to warm up a snack for the Governor.

Sandy opted, however, not to serve the Governor "rat on a plate," knowing that no joke played on the Governor would be worth any laugh one might get. Jesse Ventura liked to laugh at anyone but himself.

The Governor's son Tyrel had a more affable sense of humor and laughed along with all of us at the rubber rat race that was ensuing throughout the mansion. Since he was in on the fun, staff naturally brought him in on the horror as well and put the rubber rat in a box of Cocoa Puffs, Tyrel's favorite breakfast cereal. The First Son found it there the next morning and, after a wide-eyed moment's hesitation, shared in a good laugh with all of us.

Because all of the rat sightings seemed to begin and end at Sandy, the women on staff were determined to get even. One day, instead of taking the trash out, they put all the bags in Sandy's car trunk. This stunt was even more amusing than first intended when Sandy left early that afternoon to take her 16-year-old son to get his driver's license. The instructor checked out the car, including the spare tire in the trunk, and discovered heaps of garbage piled on top of it!

We still laugh when we think of the good times we enjoyed at the Residence, and we all still smile when we remember the special moments we shared with the Venturas.

One of the most moving times for me personally came the day that I represented the Governor in comforting an injured toddler and his family. The boy, about 2, had both arms severed in a farming accident in North Dakota and was airlifted to a hospital in Minneapolis. When I heard about the incident, I suggested that the Governor go visit the couple. His Chief of Staff Steven Bosacker said the Governor would not be able to go and suggested I ask Terry. The First Lady wasn't feeling well, however, and was concerned there might be press there that she didn't want to face. I asked if it would be okay if I represented her and the Governor at the hospital. Terry approved a gift basket to take, and I did.

I was able to get in to see the parents and tell them I was there to represent the Governor. They were young, scared and so appreciative. We hugged and cried together. It was a moving experience that showed me what the true power of a public office could be. I am certain that the Governor never really knew about the incident, even though he got the credit (as he should have since I was there representing him).

Another memorable time happened in the spring of 1999 when I approached the gates one morning and saw a group of children in front of the Residence. One little 8-year-old boy came up to my car, peeked in the window and asked if I was someone important. I was struck that, at such a tender age, he already knew that some people counted more than others. I was happy when I thought of a quick reply, "We're all important, especially you." His brown eyes got very wide and sparkled as he responded, "Really?" Then he said, "Tell Jesse that Tyrel said 'hello!'" I was excited to tell him that the Governor's son was also named Tyrel and I would let the Governor know that he said "hi." The little boy shouted "cool" at me over his shoulder as he returned to his classmates, and when I did relay the story to the Governor, he smiled too.

Perhaps the most memorable and emotional event for all of us was the 25th wedding anniversary celebration and vow renewal that Jesse and Terry Ventura celebrated at the Residence July 22, 2000. They were married July 18, 1975, three days after "The Body's" 24th birthday because Jesse Ventura had always said that he would never get married until he was at least 24 years old.

All of the original wedding party members participated in the renewal ceremony, along with the Ventura children. Tyrel served as best man; Jade was maid of honor. Minnesota State Supreme Court Justice Kathleen Blatz presided over the ceremony, and Terry Ventura's father walked her down the aisle.

Terry even wore her original wedding gown, still as slender as 25 years earlier. The First Lady was breathtaking as she descended the grand stairway, which staff had decorated with ivy and white flowers. Terry carried a beautiful bouquet of spring flowers that Theresa had made. We had lined her walkway with rose petals.

The ceremony was held around the backyard fountain, where a misty-eyed Governor presented his wife with a four-karat diamond ring. Jesse Ventura, we learned, could not afford a ring when they were first married and intended to more than make up for it after 25 years. The stone was so big his bride confessed that she was afraid the ring would drop off her finger when she worked in the barn.

Anyone who saw the Venturas exchange their vows, who saw the way they looked at each other with tears in both their eyes, could never doubt the love they share.

A small reception followed at the Residence for family members, hosted by staff. That evening we hosted a larger gathering to include additional family and guests. No staff attended.

Among the wedding photos taken, the First Couple insisted on a photo with the Residence staff, the extended family who had shared in—and in many ways made possible—such a beautiful and memorable day.

Staff put a lot of work into another memorable, personal occasion for the Venturas, the 50th birthday party the First Lady threw for her husband July 15, 2001.

Terry wanted to surprise her husband with a grand party and solicited the staff's help. The First Lady was paying for the event, and all the staff volunteered their time to make it happen.

We began planning for a Polynesian-style party in the backyard months in advance, taking pains to ensure the Governor never suspected what was being planned around him. I was at the Ventura's Maple Grove home on occasions when the Governor came home and we hid what we were working on so as not to spoil the surprise.

The Governor had a speaking engagement in Canada and returned to Minnesota on Friday afternoon. Unfortunately, he arrived home an hour early and ran into Steve Strong, a friend and fellow former wrestler, so we were afraid he might have suspected something. One thing is certain, he never suspected how big a something was awaiting him!

I had sought the help of event companies that turned the backyard and terrace into a Polynesian island paradise, complete with thatched huts, flaming torches and bamboo decorations. Our chefs outdid themselves with an exotic menu, including a stuffed pig, fresh fruits and a variety of Hawaiian dishes. An open bar and a cigar bar were favorite attractions.

My wife was commissioned to bake a huge birthday cake, complete with edible flowers and lit sparklers. The solarium was filled with a montage of memorabilia from the Governor's childhood days, his Navy tour, his wrestling and movie careers, and his years as Governor, including newspaper articles headlining his victories.

The guest list included Hollywood celebrities, government officials, professional athletes and boyhood friends. Celebrity guests included Sean Penn and actress wife, Robin Wright and their two children; actor Eric Braeden; author Harvey Mackay; NBA star Kevin KG Garnet; and Steve Strong, a tag-team buddy from their pro wrestling days. Al and Tipper Gore were invited but were in Europe at the time.

Strong presented the Governor with a special gift that night, a painting of the Governor on horseback, dressed in a suit of armor. Jesse Ventura loved the painting so much that he wanted to commission its artist to paint his official portrait for the Capitol. We hoped that the official portrait would not depict him as a regal knight in shining armor, though it was clear that Jesse Ventura liked himself painted that way.

Each guest arrived at the party without incident, except for soap opera star Eric Braeden, a.k.a. Victor on the Governor's favorite soap opera, *The Young and The Restless*. The Governor kept his schedule clear and returned home from the capitol nearly each noon hour to watch his favorite soap. He asked not to be interrupted and liked the show so much that, while Governor, Jesse Ventura made two guest appearances on the show. Braeden was one of the Governor's favorites on the soap and was a great surprise for the birthday party.

The actor had graciously invited me to lunch before the party because I'd spoken to him on the phone so many times to arrange hotel and transportation for him. I was too swamped with final details to go to lunch but did promise to pick up the gift that he had bought for the Governor, a portable weight lifting set. When I arrived at his hotel, I was amused to see the housekeeper giving Eric a difficult time about entering his room. She was questioning his identity, but I assured her that he was Eric Braeden and that he was in St. Paul as a guest of the Governor. Satisfied, the housekeeper left, and Eric confessed that, "This happens all the time. People don't believe me when I say who I am!"

Eric and the other guests soon arrived at the Residence, dressed in Hawaiian attire. Many wore leis, and we presented each lady with an orchid to wear in her hair. The First Lady wore flowers in her hair and a brightly colored long skirt with slits up the side. She looked every bit the island princess, and the Governor was enamored when he saw her and all she had pulled over on him.

The party was a great success and lasted into the early morning hours. Cleanup took several days. The Governor said it was the best surprise he had ever had.

Staff agreed the surprises that night were great indeed. Before the entertainment commenced, Jesse, Terry, Tyrel and Jade released five white doves as a symbol of long life and health for the Governor. An authentic Hawaiian band entertained guests with festive, lively music throughout the evening.

But the highlight—or "lowlight," depending on your vantage point—was watching the Governor, dressed in a grass skirt, doing the hula and rubbing noses with an Hawaiian dancer! It was over-the-top fun and funny, Ventura style. The Governor seemed drunk, not on Mai Tais, but on love, fun and power.

The Governor shined in the moonlight like any other limelight he stepped into, even in a grass skirt.

Once the torches went out, however, a different Governor emerged. The vibrant entertainer most people recognize as Jesse Ventura reverted into the reclusive, sullen, short-spoken and moody man the Residence staff knew all too well.

CHAPTER 4

JESSE: THE RECLUSE

There was more to living in the People's House than having a few guests over for dinner now and then, and the Governor hated it. This may come as a shock to those who think of Jesse Ventura as a great entertainer but, in reality, he is a loner. From the beginning of his term, the seemingly outgoing Governor tried to avoid nearly every fund-raiser, dinner and special event held at the Governor's Residence. On a good day, the Governor tolerated having a daily social life to keep up with, but most days he bowed out—and not always gracefully.

The First Lady knew that the Governor was the main attraction everyone wanted to see and knew better than anyone how difficult a task it was to get him to appear. On the days of the mansion fund-raisers, for example, the Governor would be visibly aggravated and grumpy and would hardly speak to anyone.

Terry would eventually talk him into his tuxedo and down the stairs to attend, though even she didn't always succeed. After their first year in office, she succeeded less and less.

Despite the fussing, an agitated Jesse Ventura would sometimes appear. Once in the crowd, the Governor would flip the switch on his personality. Then, it was show time for Jesse "The Entertainer."

The Governor would get on a roll telling stories and soon find his social groove. He enjoyed the limelight so much that, ironically, he was often the last person to leave. Many times, staff would be completely finished with the cleanup and would just hang around waiting for the Governor to go upstairs so they could finally go home.

I can think of no better example of how determined the Governor was not to attend social events than when the Governor's Residence Council held a November 2001 celebration of the restoration of the Steinway grand piano. Though Schmidt's Music donated its best craftsman and much of the restoration work, $10,000 was still needed to pay all the costs and the council hoped to raise the difference that evening.

Terry was the official hostess to 100 guests who paid to enjoy a concert by world-renowned Steinway artists Paul Shaw and Butch Thompson. To accommodate them and showcase the piano, we moved all furniture out of the main floor, set up seating in the dining room, solarium, and drawing room and placed the piano where every guest could see it under the chandelier in the grand foyer.

The elegant evening was wonderful in every way—a far cry from the Governor's graceless harangue over his invitation to it.

The Governor had been invited to attend, even though we all knew he probably would not. After all, he let it be emphatically known several times prior to mailing the invitations that, indeed, he would not attend. The First Lady did not even try to change his mind.

On the day of the reception, however, someone misinformed the Governor that his name was on the invitation, the equivalent of a written promise to those invited that he would appear. The Governor was furious and called the First Lady to convey his anger.

When Terry finished speaking with the Governor, she called me. She was obviously upset, thinking that I had somehow allowed the Governor's name to be included in the written invitation. She asked me if I was trying to get her divorced. I read her a copy of the invitation showing that the Governor's name was mentioned nowhere. She was relieved but said I would have to fix everything with the Governor. I silently wished myself good luck.

I knew he would be coming home for lunch to watch his soap opera, a daily ritual we were not supposed to interrupt, so I met him at the door. Upon seeing me, the Governor pointed his finger in my face and growled, "You know my policy!"

"Yes, sir," I responded. "I know how you feel about attending fund-raising events. I think you have been misinformed." I read him the invitation and, thankfully, he calmed down. The Governor stressed that he had already helped raise more than $50,000 for the Residence. I corrected his numbers to let him know the amount was more than $75,000. Satisfied, he marched upstairs to get his lunch and catch *The Young and The Restless*.

As we expected, the Governor did not appear at the grand piano fund-raiser that night.

After three mansion fund-raising events, the Governor let everyone know he was finished. He wanted nothing else to do with fund-raising because, he explained, he had done his part to raise money for the Residence while the Legislature had done nothing to appropriate funds for improvements.

In reality, I think the Governor was less concerned about the Legislature's contribution to the mansion's coffers than he was bothered by his own shyness. Though the Governor is self-centered, and the world and everyone's schedule certainly revolves around him, Jesse Ventura lacks the ability–or perhaps the confidence, or both,–to live up to the image he created for the world.

THE NO SHOW SHOWMAN

Jesse Ventura is a personality dichotomy. The over-the-top, outgoing Governor everyone sees on television is not the man most of us lived with at the Residence. Jesse "The Man" Ventura is reclusive and moody. More than anything else, he prefers to be alone in his room or with just his family or one or two friends. As much as he was a public persona, he hated being a public man.

Though the Governor could certainly appear to be warm and gracious, such expressions were usually on his own terms and rarely in the public favor. Even the Capitol staff voiced concerns that the Governor lacked good social graces and was just plain rude to the people who elected him.

Real or imagined, Jesse Ventura often gave the appearance of being self-serving, a trait that hurt his reputation and concerned those who believed in him.

For example, staff often arranged bus trips to various communities around the state so citizens could get to know the Governor better. The danger, of course, was that some people got to know the wrong side of the Governor as I witnessed at one small town high school we visited. The Governor's press person introduced the principal to the Governor. Jesse Ventura's greeting? "So?"

Later, the same staffer introduced the school's head custodian and told the Governor that the man had reported to work at four o'clock in the morning to prepare for the Governor's visit. Jesse Ventura's reply had me thinking that career politicians might not be so bad after all. "So what? I was up at 5."

His lack of social graces only got worse at home. I cannot count the number of times I had to make excuses for him because he was not in the mood to be public. I'd say things like, "You'll have to excuse the Governor for leaving early," "...not being here," "...being short with you," and on and on. Then, I'd add, "Things didn't go well at the Capitol today," or "He had a long meeting last night," or "He's not feeling well," and on and on.

If confronted directly by someone who wanted to meet the Governor, shake his hand or get his autograph, even if he was standing right there in front of them, the Governor would say "It's not on my schedule." One time, a group from Sweden had brought a special book to give the Governor, and the Governor wouldn't even accept it as he walked past. I dashed after him and explained they had something to present to him. Again he said, "It's not on my schedule." I pleaded, "Governor, it will only take a minute," and he reluctantly accepted the book and quickly went upstairs.

Such actions, or should I say inactions, always made me cringe, but I felt especially ashamed for Minnesota that the Governor had represented the state in that way to someone from another country.

Jesse Ventura's own scheduler would often lament to me about the Governor's lack of desire for personal appearances, saying: "He got elected; he should do his job."

But, as the months and lack of appearances went by, staff began to get the impression that the Governor viewed the Residence more as a place to serve his needs and image than as a place where he, as governor, served the state's needs and image.

For example, I was at a loss for satisfactory apologies when the Governor decided not to attend the reception for University of Minnesota guest lecturer Dr. Barry Levy. People had seen the Governor come in and go upstairs and couldn't understand why he would not come down for just a few minutes to say hello. This was a sore spot with many groups who had invited the Governor to appear at their event. But his reaction was typical Jesse Ventura. The man just did not like doing what he did not want to do and would duck such events at every opportunity. Most likely, he was upstairs watching television while his guests were craning their necks toward the entryway throughout the evening in hopes that Jesse Ventura just might grace them with his gubernatorial presence. It rarely happened.

As part of completing my master's degree, I taught a hospitality course at Normandale College in Bloomington, Minn., and brought the class to the Residence for a tour. The Governor's scheduler arranged for him to greet the group. We waited 15 minutes for him to come downstairs. He never did and soon left by the back door to go to his Maple Grove home. The Governor never apologized nor offered an explanation for his disappearance even though, in this case, the event was on his schedule. One student commented, "I guess he is too busy to talk to us." Silently, I thought, "His boa must be on too tight. Either that or Victor is up to no good again on *The Young and the Restless*."

I was probably most embarrassed when the Governor shunned people, especially children who were standing right in front of the man who had an action figure toy made in his image.

A day that especially stands in a bad light was the afternoon he was scheduled to be photographed with a championship Minnesota cheerleading team. All of the girls were excitedly waiting for their moment with the Governor and were extra enthused about meeting a national sports figure. Unfortunately for the teenagers, their Governor was in a terrible mood that day. He came in and never said one word to any of them, not even a mumbled "congratulations." He just grunted and stood in the middle of the group. As soon as the shot snapped, he turned and walked up stairs.

The girls just stared at me as if to ask, "What was that?" I whispered some excuse about the Governor having "a lot on his mind" but could not really think of anything sufficient to say.

After a year of making apologies, it is painful to say that the Governor became an embarrassment, even to me. I got tired of trying to cover up the Governor's rude behavior toward many of the guests visiting the People's House. In response to his grunts and shrugs toward those so eager to meet him, I simply started saying, "You'll have to excuse the Governor," and leaving it at that, without explanation, because I could not think of any more. I had reached the point where I thought, "I don't care who he is, the Governor should be civil to these people who came here to meet him. The people he served as Governor deserved something more than a grunt or a no-show!"

GRUNTS & NODS

So did the staff who served him.

The Governor stayed at the mansion more than any other Ventura except his son. As the years wore on, the First Lady and their daughter stayed more often at their Maple Grove home and would come to the mansion when schedules demanded. The Governor usually stayed at the Residence throughout the week and went home on weekends.

Though he was there more nights than not, especially the first three years, staff barely knew they had a tenant. If the Governor had not been hungry, staff would hardly have encountered him. He rarely wandered the mansion and generally was seen buzzing through on his way upstairs or on his way out the door.

The Governor spent most of his time upstairs watching TV and didn't socialize a lot either in the mansion or outside of it. When the family was there, the Venturas did occasionally welcome other couples to visit or stay overnight at the Residence. Occasionally, he might have an old friend or two over to watch a football game on the big screen. Or, his agent, writer or an attorney would come over to meet with him, but outside of official guests of the state, Jesse Ventura had few friends visiting him at the Residence. He did, however, like to golf and spent so much time on the course that security took to calling the golf course the "northern field office."

When his personal schedule was up to him, Jesse Ventura not only preferred to be alone but to be *left* alone.

The Governor would generally acknowledge staff with a head

nod or smile (the size and sincerity of which depended on his mood), but he rarely engaged in small talk and never inquired about any staff's personal matters, opinions or how their day was going. He would certainly say "hello," but there were times you wouldn't get a reply to a simple salutation. He was civil to us, at least most of the time, but no one would ever call Jesse Ventura "chatty."

Temporary staffs were often brought up short by the Governor's seemingly hostile behavior. The state painters charged with applying all those coats of pink to the First Couple's bedroom found it hard to get so much as a "good morning" from the Governor, who would often sit in the room and ignore them while they painted. The only conversation they had with him over the course of several days was when he asked them what was taking so long (when in fact they were waiting for the First Lady to finish her paint selections). The long-tenured state painters confided to Residence staff how unusual it was not to be able to banter with the boss. Past governors, without exception, always made small talk with the painters—at least in passing—when they were working. Yet, nearly without fail, Governor Ventura passed them by, as if no one was there at all.

The Governor's rudeness extended to guests in the mansion. For example, the Governor was rude to KS95 Radio personalities "Van & Cheryl" when they helped to host one of our Halloween Open House festivities, an event they volunteered to do as a favor to Terry, who had been a frequent guest on their show. At one point, Van went upstairs to a setting room we'd reserved for breaks and walked by the Governor on his way. Van said "hello," and received the standard gubernatorial grunt in reply. Van was so taken back by the Governor's rudeness that I heard him comment about it several times on the air.

When you're living with a difficult person, you learn to walk on eggshells, and if one cracked, look out! The staff knew, for example, not to try a practical joke on the Governor, not to throw unexpected things on his schedule, not to touch his cigars or run out of ice cream sandwiches.

We also learned early on that if you wanted a conversation with him, you had to start it. If you wanted to flip the switch on the Governor's mood, you had to ask him a question about himself that he wanted to answer, something that made him feel validated, such as asking for his comment on the Legislature or the media. For example, if I'd say, "Good morning Governor, congratulations on passing the budget!" he would respond and tell me what he thought about it and thank me for the compliment. But if I said, "Good morning, Governor, beautiful day isn't it?" he'd grunt an affirmative and keep walking. We learned that if you got a grunt, it was a good day. We felt sometimes we were the peasants and he the king who addressed us only when needed or if he was in a particularly good mood.

The Governor was so awkward in his personal conversations that we suspected the only one he talked to more, and more intimately, outside of his family was his dog, Franklin. That bulldog actually heard full sentences from the Governor every day.

Governor Ventura also disliked being touched (by anyone but his wife, of course; he liked her a lot). He'd certainly offer and return a handshake or jab if someone tossed one his way, but friendly pats on the back or hugs—like those our gregarious Sylvia readily gave out to everyone that visited—made him uncomfortable.

I believe his aversion to human contact contributed to his reaction to a touching incident during a March 2000 TV debate with Representative Carol Molnau. "She put her hand on my thigh, grasped my arm, put her hand on my shoulder and patted me on the back.... I was very uncomfortable with being touched like that," the Governor later told his weekly radio audience. His discomfort, he added, was that the politician's touches bordered on sexual harassment. "I'm sorry, Governor, if I hurt you," Rep. Molnau responded in the *Minneapolis Star Tribune* March 25, 2000. "I didn't know you were that fragile."

The Governor was equally uneasy when any kind of emotion was presented, or worse, when he was asked to express any of the softer emotions. The former wrestler just wasn't comfortable expressing feelings like appreciation, love or friendship toward individuals or intimate groups.

The deeper the emotion, the bigger the struggle it seemed. He especially lacked appropriate graces when the Venturas visited Terry's dying grandmother in the hospital. His security detail later told me how embarrassed they'd been by the Governor's actions at the hospital where he spent much of the time talking about himself and joking with security. They were surprised by his loud and uncouth behavior, given the graveness and sadness of the situation. Their story only added to my theory that Jesse Ventura was unable to look beyond himself and largely unable to sympathize with other people.

Even in more businesslike settings, the Governor found emotions hard to express. For example, at the first staff appreciation/holiday party, the Governor was supposed to talk to the staff and thank us for our service. He literally just mumbled a few things, sort of a "thanks guys" approach. Fortunately, the First Lady jumped in with the more gracious show of appreciation that the Governor was too uncomfortable to display.

CHAPTER 5

TERRY: THE PEOPLE'S LADY

When Terry Ventura heard that her husband had just been elected Governor of Minnesota, she cried in her mother's arms. They were not tears of joy.

Jesse Ventura had wanted the job—or at least he wanted to win the title—of Governor. His wife never wanted to be First Lady. She liked the job she had with her horse farm and her children. She preferred living a step away from center stage. Yet, when her husband's ambitions thrust the spotlight upon her, Terry Ventura outshined her husband at every turn.

If a victory story can be salvaged from the Ventura reign over Minnesota, it is the transformation of Terry Ventura from reticent wife, mother and businesswoman into confident speaker, entertainer and popular First Lady. Terry grew a whole lot more as a person, and rose closer to her potential, than her husband did while he was Governor. The timid and insecure hostess we first met in 1999 blossomed in the gubernatorial limelight into a passionately poised political butterfly.

Terry Ventura only gained confidence in her abilities, and herself, as she added experience to her role as First Lady.

In the first few months, Terry would often call me and ask me about a hairstyle or a dress she wanted to wear and was especially concerned about what people thought of her appearance and performance. She felt as if she were on a giant pedestal, standing there for public scrutiny. It was a feeling only fueled by the fact that she really was on a giant pedestal of public scrutiny.

We received dozens of calls from so-called experts, and hundreds of calls and letters from Minnesotans, with opinions on everything from what Terry should wear to how she should cut her hair. Rarely did anyone comment on what she should say or do, just on how she looked. The most often expressed opinion was that she should stop wearing the sleeveless shirts she wore when she was riding horses. The constant barrage of fashion opinion was enough to make even me start second-guessing my suit and tie!

Eventually, the First Lady, learned to take such criticism with scarcely a blink and lived life with her own style, sleeveless shirts and all. Terry soon became the confident, personable First Lady the public and staff admired.

I traveled with her often to public events, and she always came across well in speeches. People connected with her right away. The Governor was probably better with one-liners than his wife, but the First Lady was more adept than the Governor at giving long speeches. Terry Ventura can connect with an audience on a deeper, more personal level by tying in personal stories and examples that made people naturally relate to her.

She was, however, a reluctant speaker and critical of her own performance. When we traveled, she would always ask me to listen to her as she practiced and to try to boost her confidence. I always felt that she did great, but she was her own worst critic. She would come off a stage and say, "I'm never doing that again!" Sometimes she meant it. If another speaker or a host said something critical of her husband, Terry Ventura would often refuse to speak for that group again.

THE REAL GOVERNOR

Though competent in public, Terry Ventura's best work was in the behind-the-scenes details that her husband never thought about. In nearly every way, and nearly every day, Terry Ventura was the better governor.

Terry was the better political game player. She knew what to say to whom and when and how to best say it. More importantly, she knew what not to say and when and to whom. She thought about the consequences of what she said before she said it. She considered how people would feel and react over something she did or said. The Governor rarely considered consequences, unless it involved himself. She was a long-term strategist; he was a knee-jerk reactionist.

The First Lady was also the Governor's conscious; some say his only real heart. When the Governor misspoke, or didn't speak at all, it was the First Lady who found the right words on his behalf, the First Lady who sent letters of explanation.

Terry also has more heart and more compassion for others than the Governor did. She could be extremely gracious and kind, loving and sympathetic. Or, at least, she was very good at conveying such emotions convincingly.

The First Lady has a special love for children, and she regularly did charity work to help raise money for children's needs. It was always an especially moving experience to accompany the First Lady when she visited children in local hospitals. Terry always had tears in her eyes after visiting the children. She'd hold their hand, tease and laugh with them, and try to make them smile.

Though these were often emotionally trying visits, Terry usually found a way to make everyone laugh. On one occasion, it was a young boy we were visiting who brought the house down. He had recently been through chemotherapy and was as bald as the Governor. Since I was with Terry, he thought I was Jesse Ventura. In all sincerity, he said, "You have more hair in person!"

The First Lady had a quick and warm sense of humor that often came out when she joked with staff. She kidded me in particular about keeping my office too neat and clean. One morning, I arrived early to find that the First Lady and her assistant had literally trashed my office. Terry left a tongue-in-cheek note on my desk, which read, "As much as I admire your skill as Residence manager, your office is very unprofessional. Please have it in proper order by the time I come in today!"

Terry also took time to know not only the names of all the staff, their spouses and children but to know the staff themselves a little. She asked how we were and how our families were and seemed to care genuinely about the answer. The First Lady often took time writing staff thank you notes and letters. (See examples page 74.) The Governor rarely called anyone but me by name and never inquired about staff's family.

Because of the personal relationship we felt with her, staff cared about Terry and her well-being. We were all especially concerned for her, and grieved with her, through the losses of her father, grandmother and stepmother while the Venturas were in office. We did all that we could think to do to make the death easier to bear for the First Lady and her children. For example, the First Lady's stepmother fell gravely ill during the Venturas' first tax season in office. Terry was trying to push past her grief to get the family's tax information collected and mailed. It was after 11 p.m., and Terry had not yet mailed the tax information. I was still at the Residence, working on events for the next day, and I volunteered to take the completed forms to the nearest post office. After three stops, I found a post office still open. Terry's stepmother died a few days later.

Any of us would have done something extra like that to make the First Lady's life at the Residence easier. Terry Ventura was the kind of down-to-earth, approachable person anyone would want to serve.

Her ability to relate to people was probably best showcased at the first staff appreciation party Jan. 14, 2000. Not only did she smooth over the Governor's brief thank you with gracious and gushing words of her own, the First Lady proved to the 100 Capitol and Residence staff present that she could party like a good old girl. She brought in a surprise 50th birthday cake for me and got into the rhythms of the Singing Express female vocal group hired as the night's entertainment. The First Lady even got staff to sing karaoke with her, including a rendition of Tammy Wynette's "Stand By Your Man"—a song about loyalty no matter what, which we all agreed privately should have been the Venturas' personal anthem.

The fun, genuine lady we saw that night was Terry's best side. In time, we would come to know that the First Lady had a steely side as well. Terry Ventura is an intelligent and determined businesswoman who studies up on the issues and problems and uses her abilities and personalities to get what she wants. The First Lady is also steadfastly protective of her friends and family and a tough adversary in an argument. When she got riled up over something she was passionate about, Terry could be formidable. If she was defending someone she loved, like her children, she could be fingernails on a chalkboard.

And, the First Lady, knew how to play her trump card. Whenever she really wanted something she would say, "After all, I am married to the boss."

Terry Ventura
First Lady

Dear Dan & Jan —
Thank you for all your help at the fishing opener. I heard you had to leave Saturday evening and I was so sorry to hear it. You were both _fantastic_ and very _professional_! My family also thanks you. Next year a little simpler program I hope! God Bless, Terry & Jesse & Jade

A LETTER OF PRAISE FROM TERRY

Terry Ventura wrote the following letter about me, and about the closing of the Residence, to a reporter at the *St. Cloud Times* in March 2002, just about six weeks before the Governor's Residence closed. It was a handwritten note, and I have typed it here as written.

Dear Ms. Gustafson,

I am sorry but this is the soonest I could answer your message and questions. My computer printer if on the blink so my scratching will have to do.

Dan came to the Residence in early 1999 and during the time before that, it was my assistant Mari, me and a friend Amy who answered calls, organized mail, made up a filing (crudely!) system and tried to keep everything going. Dan came in and really pulled an office together very quickly. He is a good organizer and has a way of getting people to work together and feel like they are part of a special team.

I wanted the Residence to run as efficiently as possible fiscally. Dan got us a property tax break, found vendors and ways to save money that really impressed the Governor's office.

Dan also has a wonderful sense of style and elegance. He knows how to pull a room together. I have stressed that the Residence always combine stately elegance with a warm homey fell. He has found the correct balance. He combines works of art with personal

I am very concerned about the staff and
have already begun trying to find n
jobs for them. We are like a worke
family

wonde

would

own in

are fo

I bel

ot ch

staff a

work to

the ver

Do

Poise,

made

I will

family photos and arranges furniture to make cozy place to chat.

Everyone who arrives for an official function or a family get together is greeted by Dan or a staff member at the door and always leaves with a personal "goodbye, please come back again soon!"

Personally, Dan is warm, witty, has a great sense of humor, enjoys receiving and giving helpful advice. He can take a practical joke and can give it right back again. He can play piano beautifully and loves to dance with his beautiful wife Jan. He is a very committed family man and enjoys traveling.

Dan and I have been a great team. I come up with ideas and he fine tunes them and makes them happen. He is well connected in all parts of the community and can always find someone to get what I want done.

For the Governor's 50th birthday, I gave him the task of turning the Residence into the Governor's favorite vacation spot. Hawaii was created right on Summit Avenue. We had tiki huts, fire dancers, a Hawaiian band, hula dancers, exotic birds and Jan, his wife, made the most extraordinary layer cake with real flowers and sparklers on the top! Everyone who attended really believed they were in the islands!

Dan knows protocol backwards and forwards. He always knows exactly how to prepare the Residence for visiting dignitaries and to make them feel right at ease.

As to the closing of the Residence, we are

all heartbroken. The cuts to the budget of the Governor's office by the legislature are devastating. In January as the Governor and his staff were preparing their budget plan to present to Minnesota and the legislature, we were told to eliminate two staff positions and cut $16,000 from our budget at the Residence. We only have a staff of 10 people and we already ran a lean financial operations so these cuts hit us hard. Dan and I fought as hard as we could to keep our staff but the recession and the attacks on 9-11-01 were making the financial climate of the state budget very bleak.

The legislature came in session a few weeks latter and cut the Governor's office even more. (They had already cut their office by 13% and lost several staff members when we did in January)

This was a crushing blow. The legislature did not accept the Governor's office budget, which would have kept everything open and running (albeit on a very tight financial rein) and had all departments make financial cuts at the same time. With the legislature's budget and new cuts, the Governor's Administration budget could no longer afford the cost of keeping the Residence open. You cannot run an operation of that size with fewer people and less money than we already did.

It was a very sad decision to have to make. Dan and I have worked very hard to make the Residence what it is today. The Governor and

I am very concerned about the staff and have already begun trying to find new jobs for them. We are like a worke... family... wonder... would... own im... are fo... I bel... ot cha... staff at... work to... the ver... Dan... Poise,... made... I will

myself have done a lot of private fund raising to improve and redecorate. We have had wonderful support from the 1006 Society and the Governor's Residence Council for everything from refurbishing the glorious Steinway Grand Piano to adding a whole new dinnerware set with the official state seal emblem on it.

I am very concerned about the staff and have already begun trying to find new jobs for them. We are like a working family. I have had many sleepless nights wondering where they will go or what they would do.

Times are hard all over for our state. My own immediate family have lost jobs or are facing company cut backs and shut downs.

I believe better times are ahead. I would not change a minute I have spent with my staff at the Residence. I will continue to work to find them help, jobs and wish them the very best.

Dan Creed is a very unique blend of class, warmth, poise, humor, intelligence, and kindness that has made our working together an experience I will always remember fondly.

I hope this covers all your questions. Thank you for your interest.

Sincerely,
Terry Ventura

P.S. How did St. Cloud come out from the storm? I was out plowing our farm out with the Governor until 11:30 p.m. last night!

CHAPTER 6

JESSE: THE BLOWHARD

When the First Lady wasn't able to save him, the Governor's reactions blew up in his face. In the end, it was what Governor Ventura said that brought his reign to a controversial and disappointing finish.

Jesse Ventura had shock value, an in-your-face style. For a while, people liked it and thought his was a refreshing approach to politics. They saw their new Governor as quick-witted and fast with a comeback. He was, in fact, great in the one-line debate.

I remember an incident in 1999 when 300 protestors marched to the Residence to let the Governor know they wanted extended welfare payments. As the Governor prepared to leave for the Capitol that morning, I mentioned the protestors' anticipated arrival later in the day and asked if there was anything he wanted me to say to them. He said but one sentence, "Tell them to get a job."

When the marchers arrived, I tempered the Governor's greeting, but only a little. I was standing outside by the fence with several state troopers when the protesters reached the house. A large, young man yelled across the fence to me, "Who are you? Jesse's boy?" I assured him I was nobody's boy. When he asked where the Governor was, I told him, "He is working, where you should be as well!" I later conveyed the story to the Governor who smiled in pleasure at our retort.

In this case, the one-liner worked. More often, the Governor's propensity to speak his mind, regardless of the consequences, backfired with the kind of political collateral damage that cannot be rebuilt.

The reality is that a wrestler and candidate can get away with saying whatever he wants, but a Governor has to temper himself a bit. And, "temper" is something Governor Ventura only knows how to lose, not restrain.

Perhaps long-time Ventura critic and well-known Minnesota author Garrison Keillor summarized the Governor's style best when he described Jesse Ventura as a "...mutha who talks in a steroid growl and doesn't stop."

I'm not sure this book is large enough to include all of the Governor's colorful and controversial growls, but there were several verbal punches that I believe landed Jesse Ventura in the hottest water.

Some Minnesotans were not amused when he called Hillary Clinton a "circus sideshow act" and when he came down on a recently widowed welfare mother, telling her to "shut up and get a job." Critics questioned the wisdom of his decision to play a corrupt Governor on his favorite TV Soap Opera, *The Young and The Restless*.

Those familiar with the Governor's own blowhard commentary thought it paradoxical when he asked President George W. Bush and Assistant Secretary of State Otto Reich to apologize after the secretary said in September 2002 that he hoped those traveling to Cuba for an agribusiness convention (which included the Venturas) would not engage in the country's "sexual tourism." The Governor, who issued insults like proclamations in Minnesota, called the secretary's remark "offensive" and demanded that the president "owes my wife and children a personal apology," reported the Associated Press on Sept. 10, 2002.

Many thought the Governor hit a foul note when, just hours after students had died in the Littleton, Colo., school shooting in May 1999, the Governor said the incident "supports conceal and carry," while other leaders were offering thoughts and condolences

Minnesota morals were tested when the newly elected Governor—whose famed wrestling slogan had been "win if you can, lose if you must, but always cheat,"—whined that the *St. Paul Pioneer Press* should have held its March 1999 expose (which revealed that 20 University of Minnesota basketball players had cheated on tests) until after the NCAA tournament so that the Gophers could have participated.

Moral ears really started burning when the Governor's admissions put the Minnesota name forever on the seedier maps of Nevada. After the Governor's book, *I Ain't Got Time to Bleed*, recounted his 1970 visit to a Nevada brothel, an entrepreneurial brothel owner posted a sign in front of his Moonlight Bunny Ranch that read, "Governor Jesse Ventura had sex here,"—and encouraged customers "to wrestle where Jesse did."

Even the Irish were against him! Emerald Isle descendants took offense when Jesse Ventura rumbled to talk show host David Letterman in early 1999 about how drunken Irishmen had screwed up the crooked streets of St. Paul.

Everyone was generally confused over why the Governor of the state of Minnesota didn't have time to vote in the Sept. 10, 2002, primary election. I knew his schedule that day, and it was admittedly tight with meetings. Yet, it was not so tight that the Governor couldn't take in a Minnesota Twins baseball game with a charity group that night. (Polls in Minnesota are open until 8 p.m.) That was also the day, according to a February 2003 *St. Paul Pioneer Press* article by Jim Ragsdale that the Governor posted an 18-hole golf score on a computerized Web site. The controversy surrounding the Governor's ballot no-show led Minnesotans to the discovery that Sept. 10 was not the first time that Jesse Ventura had not completed his most basic civic duty. When then candidate Ventura voted in the Sept. 15, 1998, gubernatorial primary, it was the first time he had voted since 1994. (That means he didn't get to the polls to cast a vote for U.S. Senate Candidate Dean Barkley when Jesse Ventura was the Reform Party candidate's campaign chairman, noted *Minneapolis Star Tribune* reporter Mark Brunswick Oct. 2, 2002.)

The Governor found plenty of time a week later, however, to accept an award from Kids Voting Minnesota, a group that educates children about exercising their right to vote. I readily agreed with the Governor when I heard him tell the children: "Do you know that in the United States, only 50 percent of adults vote? That's pathetic."

The Governor lost the favor of hunters as well—a large group in Minnesota—when he cut down their sport and pumped up his own Rambo image as he responded to criticism of his fishing and hunting stands in an April 2001 *Minneapolis Star Tribune* interview. "Until you've hunted man, you haven't hunted yet."

This statement especially disturbed me as the son of a combat veteran. I have never known any veterans to refer to their orders to track and kill the enemy as the sport of "hunting man." I was even more disturbed, however, that the Governor felt it necessary to repeat this statement at least one dozen times during that interview, according to the newspaper.

A bit of my respect for the Governor slipped away that day. I had always appreciated that the Governor had given of himself as a young man to serve our country. I had felt a special bond with him on the subject of military service ever since I read that his father, like mine, had been a World War II veteran.

The Governor only learned the details of his father's service after his dad died and was shocked and proud to learn that his father had won "seven bronze battle stars" in the war. It was a pride we shared in that my father too is a war hero. Staff Sergeant Herschel E. Creed flew 60 combat missions in North Africa and Asia, where he won not only the respect of all who served with him but the acknowledgments of a grateful nation, including the Air Medal with four bronze stars and the Distinguished Flying Cross.

The Governor's revelation that he had waited too long to ask his father the details of his service prompted me to ask my own father even more about his war experiences. So, it was because of Jesse Ventura that I learned that the man who'd always been my hero was a national hero as well. (Years later, the Governor of Kentucky presented my dad a Kentucky Colonel award, given Kentucky natives who have contributed to the betterment of the state and country.)

Listening, then, to the Governor talk about "hunting man" made me start to question the Governor's combat-seasoned persona. Though nearly all of the "war stories" I heard him tell at the Residence revolved around his Navy and commando training, and not actual combat, Jesse Ventura's legendary bravado has long perpetuated the image that he is a combat veteran like his brother Jan who served in combat with the Navy SEALS in Vietnam.

I want to state clearly that I have no doubt that Jesse Ventura (then James Janos) served our country well during the Vietnam

War, and I know firsthand how proud he is when he wears his Navy SEAL t-shirts. However, I cannot imagine a humble combat hero like my father—or his—making that kind of statement. The war veterans I know do *not* boast of their killing prowess, consider themselves to be heroes or talk of war as a sport. They flip pancakes at the American Legion breakfast, volunteer in their community, fly the flag, and talk about combat and combat training only reluctantly and then only as a part of "their job."

It's long been my understanding that America's real heroes are the quietest.

PLAYBOY BLUNDERS

For all his boisterous foibles and follies, Governor Ventura laid the biggest political egg when he exposed too many of his inner thoughts in the October 1999 issue of *Playboy Magazine*. I think many Minnesotans would agree that the most revealing image in that issue was the snapshot of the real Jesse Ventura that unfolded in its pages.

In my mind, that interview was the beginning of the end for Jesse "The Politician" Ventura because it magnified what a loud mouth the Governor could be and revealed to the masses the true insensitivities he had toward people.

Aside from reiterating his often controversial stands on legalizing prostitution and drugs, and again admitting his use of both in the past, the Governor said he could understand the Navy pilot's behavior in the Tailhook sexual harassment scandal. (Though in his book *Do I Stand Alone?*, the Governor insisted that this quote began with, "I don't condone it," public perception balanced on what people read in *Playboy*.)

He didn't win over many fans with his comments about suicide either. "If you're to the point of killing yourself and you're that depressed, life can only get better. If you're a feeble-minded person to begin with, I don't have time for you."

The most shocking line in the article was probably the Governor's postulation over what it would be like to be reincarnated as a 38-double-d bra!—an especially crude remark, even for Governor Ventura.

The most damning remark of the article hit at the heart of Minnesota and shook our state's religious foundation. The Governor of a state where some 70 percent of residents say they attend church regularly told *Playboy* that, "Religion is a sham and crutch for weak-minded people who need strength in numbers."

Reaction to Ventura's comments was strong and swift across the state and across political lines. Joan Campbell, general secretary of the National Council of Churches noted, "Karl Marx said something like that (and) I don't think he (Governor Ventura) wants to be associated with him." Merlyn Scroggins, president of the Catholic Defense League in St. Paul added, "We should feel terribly sad that we have a man of this nature as our Governor."

The Catholic League for Religious and Civil Rights went so far as to call the Governor, "Jesse 'The Bigot' Ventura," and even the national Reform Party Chairman said he was "disgusted and outraged" by the *Playboy* comments.

The ire of many Minnesotans was raised to the point that Ron Eibensteiner, chairman of the Minnesota state Republican Party, suggested that Ventura "consider stepping down."

An Oct. 8, 1999, poll by Mason-Dixon Polling and Research Inc., of Washington, D.C., revealed that 80 percent of Minnesota voters disagreed with the Governor's religious statement. Furthermore, 43 percent had changed their mind since December 1998 when they told the same pollster that Jesse Ventura was a "breath of fresh air." Less than a year later, voters said he was "an embarrassment."

The person most affected by the Governor's religious remark was, of course, *not* Jesse Ventura. It was his wife Terry because she regularly attended church. The press was hot after the First Lady to get the Missouri Synod Lutheran to admit that she was upset with her husband. In public, she stood by him even on that subject, but at home he knew she was not happy about his comments. Terry went some time without talking to her husband, something highly unusual in the Ventura household.

The press followed Terry to church to get a comment and even got into a confrontation with her security detail when some reporters tried to get a quote from the pews.

The Governor went ballistic over how the press was hounding his wife. Residence staff knew the Governor was upset because those days were some of the few times that the Governor made unsolicited comments to us in the mansion about something political. His conversations with me would generally start with, "Dan, did you read what that snake in the grass said!"

Though I never heard him admit it, I think how his wife was treated brought the Governor up short. He even tried to explain his comments, saying he hadn't intended them to sound so harsh. Religion was fine for those who needed a higher power, he said, but he did not personally need such a connection. (At the mansion, we whispered that this was probably because Jesse Ventura thought he was the higher power.)

In his later book *Do I Stand Alone?*, Jesse Ventura insists that the whole comment was misinterpreted. "I said religion was a crutch for weak minded people, but we were talking about the Religious Right and the misuse of religion in politics... (*Playboy*) didn't mention that, just the quote that sounded like I was talking about religion in general."

The Governor tried to smooth things over by sending a letter to Minnesota religious leaders and saying at a Sept. 30, 1999 press conference, that "...all religious leaders will forgive me because I think that's what religion is all about, forgiving." Had he stopped there, they might have, even though the Governor never officially asked them for forgiveness. However, the Governor made no new friends when he continued his comments with, "I haven't started any wars throughout time. Has religion?"

The religion comments dogged the Governor for the rest of his political career, and he was still trying to explain himself when political TV talk show host Chris Matthews interviewed him on Dec. 27, 1999. "That was my fault," he backpedaled, "by not saying 'some.' Had I simply said 'some religions are shams and crutches for weak-minded people, probably not much would have been made of it."

I suppose that explanation did appease "some," but "others" remained unconvinced.

I never did hear Jesse Ventura offer explanations or apologies for his other *Playboy* comments, however. So, we are left to assume that the Governor is holding fast to his dreams of being reincarnated as a 38-double-d bra.

BOILING OVER

By early spring of 2000, the Governor's habit of "saying it like it is," had brought his own staff to the boiling point. The senior team called for a private meeting at the Residence with the Governor. Chief of Staff Steven Bosacker, Director of Communications John Wodele, Director of Operations Paula Brown, Director of Policy Wendy Wustenburg, and Director of Citizen Outreach and Appointments Rachel Wobschall met the Governor in the drawing room.

The team was trying to get the Governor to curtail his "off the wall" comments, trying to get Jesse Ventura to comprehend the damage such comments could create not just for his political career but for the people around him and for the image of the state of Minnesota.

John Wodele's voice, in particular, was heard over the other team members. As communication director, it was his job to deal with the ramifications of such comments. With Governor Ventura at the state's microphone, I often thought John Wodele might be the most beleaguered communications director in Minnesota history.

The intervention proved intense. Staff voices were loud and unrestrained for much of the meeting. At times, profanity could be clearly heard streaming down the Residence hallways. At one point, a senior team member came out of the drawing room and lamented, "Dan, he just does not get it!"

That came as no surprise to my ears. I don't think that Jesse Ventura could ever comprehend how offensive some of his statements were to others. He didn't have the empathy required to comprehend it.

Some of what the senior staff said must have gotten through, however, because the Governor did seem to tone down his comments, at least for a while. Though his popularity rating hit the skids—dropping from 70 to 54 percent after the *Playboy* interview—he held his tongue long enough to bring the number back to 60-plus percent in a few months. (Eventually, it would plummet below 40 percent.)

"I can survive the crucible of public displeasure; I'm stronger than ever," he told his *Do I Stand Alone?* audience. For a little while, it looked as if the Governor might indeed survive.

The Governor's admonitions did not last long enough, however. After all, Jesse Ventura is just too loose a cannon, too prone to misfiring regardless of the impact it has on him, or others. The Governor even admitted as much in a June 19, 2002, *USA Today* article. "Will I get into someone's face? Certainly. You know, that's me. I'm not going to change who I am."

It wasn't as if the Minnesota press was in much of a mood to give the Governor any wiggle room anyway. But, then, who could blame them?

PRESSING THE 'JACKALS'

The media was the Governor's favorite punching bag. The Governor lambasted the media even early in his administration, at first for ignoring him in the campaign and then for paying too much attention to him afterwards. Many times, he would come into the Residence howling about how the media always gave their own slant to everything he would say. His general theme was that the media didn't want to report the news; they wanted to make the news.

Early on, the Governor warned journalists that they were in for a fight when he told the Society of Professional Journalists that they would be up against a warrior. "I am at an age now when I can't go out and be a warrior, so I have to be a mental one. I've got you to be my adversaries," he said.

After the *Playboy* frenzy, the Governor got especially defensive around the media and would often liken reporters to sharks who "smelled blood in the water" and circled around him waiting for a sensational bite.

In the beginning of his term as Governor, the media was optimistic and extended him a gubernatorial honeymoon. However, the press soon became critical of the Governor, especially of his personal choices of phrases and appearances. Such "personal attacks" were the itch that got the deepest under Jesse Ventura's skin. Unfortunately, "The Body" had pretty thin skin.

One reporter got off on the wrong foot just after the inaugural when he kidded the Governor about his singing of "Werewolves of London" with Warren Zevon that night. Governor Ventura took great offense to the joke and made it clear how combative the relationship with the press was going to be the next four years. "That was cute," he sneered, according to a Feb. 15, 1999, *Newsweek* article. "If you're going to criticize my singing, feel free. You criticize everything else I do."

It didn't take that reporter, or anyone who knew him, long to realize that Jesse Ventura loved to dish out criticism, but rarely could he take it well himself.

The Governor got especially angry when the press began asking questions about the money he was making while in office. When the Governor wrote two books, refereed the World Wrestling Federation SummerSlam match in Minnesota, spent Saturdays as an XFL football commentator, or took paid trips to national TV interviews, the local media repeatedly asked, "Where is the Governor?" and accused him of prostituting the office for personal gain. (Jesse Ventura, who earned about $120,000 as Governor, reportedly received more than $320,000 for the 13-week XFL gig alone. Including my $63,800 salary, the entire Residence staff certainly made far less than that in a year.)

Stories about his extracurricular money-making opportunities, especially his XFL gig, really set the Governor off. He'd come home and bellow at no one and everyone that it was "nobody's business what I do in my spare time!"

When he felt personally attacked, the Governor would turn vengeful, often from the platform of his one-hour weekly radio show, "Lunch with the Governor," on WCCO. For example, on Aug. 27, 1999, he called the *St. Paul Pioneer Press*, the "St. Paul Pioneer Porn" and accused its editors and writers of being "a bunch of hypocrites from top to bottom ... (who) are working together with the X-rated industry."

Another time in 1999, I heard him call one of his press critics a "fat load" and a "McIdiot." After columnist and radio interviewer Joe Soucheray called Jesse Ventura "Governor Turnbuckle," the Governor accused the journalist of "writing garbage about me" and refused to shake hands when Soucheray hosted the Governor on his show.

Most Minnesotans remember the time the Governor joked (or maybe he was serious) with television reporters just before the start of a Governor-led hunt that he'd give "the press a 10-minute head start, then that's what we're going to hunt."

Beyond intimidation, the Governor liked to use nuggets about reporters' lives to his advantage in an interview and would sometimes mention to me when he'd overheard a juicy tidbit to use in a future fight. Most notably, the Governor jabbed at a TV reporter about his pending divorce while he was interviewing the Governor on the air.

If a reporter asked a question the Governor disliked or had otherwise upset him, the Governor would refuse to answer any further questions or grant interviews to the reporter. After four years, there were few, if any, reporters who had escaped the Governor's shunning.

In fact, WCCO-TV's Pat Kessler noted in a December 2001 *American Journalism Review* article by Jill Rosen that the Governor turned him down 41 times in a row for an interview request. Outside of press conferences, the political reporter added, he interviewed the Governor one-on-one three times in three years. When I read that, I was not surprised because the Venturas considered Kessler a real "snake in the grass" reporter. I heard both Jesse, and especially Terry, use that phrase repeatedly at the mansion and, most often, it was with the name "Kessler" attached. I never understood the insult because I always thought Kessler was as fair as anyone else. My guess is the Venturas just didn't like that he pointed out their shortcomings. He made the mistake of disagreeing with the Governor, and disagreement meant disloyalty.

By the end of his term, Minnesota TV reporter Tom Hauser was one of the few reporters who Ventura would talk to because the Governor thought that Hauser had remained "loyal" in his writings. The Governor also liked the book Hauser wrote that highlighted his speeches, *Inside the Ropes with Jesse Ventura.*

Media bashing reached a frenzied pitch when the Governor denied local media access to his post-September 11th World Trade Center visit, giving those rights to ABC TV, which had paid for the 2001 trip. When the media used the decision for editorial fodder, the Governor declared war during his radio show, saying the press "will be running and hiding as fast as the Taliban," reported *St. Paul Pioneer Press* newsman Jim Ragsdale Jan. 3, 2003.

The Governor seemed to declare marshal law and tried to ban local media interviews all together, telling me not to expect any more interviews at the mansion, unless they were national. The Governor always liked the national press, and MSNBC's Chris Matthews and CNBC *Meet the Press* commentator Tim

Russert were among his favorites, in part because they seemed to throw the Governor "softball" questions on controversial subjects. Eventually, the Governor settled on allowing some local media interviews, provided that no tape recorders or microphones were involved.

The Governor's battle plan also called for Minnesotans to boycott local newspapers and television, a battle cry I heard him sound on his weekly radio program. For a moment I wondered if the Governor would put his money where his political mouth was and give up watching his TV soap opera as well, until he clarified that he was only asking people to boycott news programs. (Whew!)

Media inquiries irritated the Governor so much that he referred to reporters as "jackals" and to the Capitol pressroom as the "rat-infested basement." Staff rarely heard the Governor call the local press anything human. "Rats," "snakes," and "jackals" were his favorite descriptors. On press conference or interview days at the mansion, he was known to ask me, "Are the jackals here yet?"

The derogatory nickname carried further still when the Governor had Capitol staff change the official press badges it issued to read, "Media Jackal" and tried to insist that every media member wear one to get into a press event. We kept several of these badges at the mansion in case visiting media forgot theirs. I did see a few reporters wearing them, but not for long. The badges were popular with reporters ... as souvenirs.

In the end, the Governor couldn't make the badges stick, but he loved to boast about the idea, just as he loved to use every opportunity, no matter how innocent, to slam the media. I remember the day he visited a local grade school and actually did a *Saturday Night Live*-style skit where he said a word and asked the school children to repeat it. Their Governor said, "I want you all to say 'Jackals' with me." When the room full of kids gleefully shouted, "Jackals!" the Governor loved it.

Such playground tactics did not endear reporters to the Governor or his causes. Press and politicians are supposed to be adversarial in the hopes that one will keep the other "honest." However, our former Navy SEAL took the rivalry over the top and made lasting, personal enemies in the press for himself.

U.S. Vice President Al Gore and his wife Tipper made good on their family values message by joining the Venturas in attending daughter Jade's horseback riding event, held the night of the Gores' visit to Minnesota.

The tall and short of working at the Governor's Residence was quite obvious the day I tried to measure up to Minnesota Timberwolves star Kevin 'KG' Garnet.

Our brief mansion guest, Stewart Peters, buddied up to everyone at the Residence, including me (Dan Creed), to get free room and board under the guise that he was a famous actor's brother Coleman Hughes.

Two of Jesse Ventura's favorite stars: his daughter Jade and Eric Braeden, star of the Governor's favorite Soap Opera, *The Young and The Restless.*

Governor Ventura's son Tyrel looked to actor Sean Penn (shown here with his wife and daughter during the Governor's 50th birthday party) as a movie industry mentor. The seasoned actor invited the aspiring movie maker to help him on a couple of films during the Ventura Administration.

6

It was a Royal Wedding to be sure when the Residence shared in the emotional moment of Jesse and Terry Ventura's wedding vow renewal ceremony, in celebration of their 25th wedding anniversary. (The dress is the same one Terry wore when the Venturas got married in 1975.)

7

Tyrel Ventura introduces his father at the Governor's surprise 50th birthday party, which featured a Hawaiian theme complete with thatched huts and flaming torches.

8

Franklin, the Ventura's gaseous bulldog, was forever trying his best to get in on the act, get in under foot or just get in a good nap.

9

Yes. A former Navy SEAL slept in this master bedroom at the Residence, at least the room's hues matched the pink boa he wore during his pro wrestling days and still sometimes hung in the bedroom closet.

10

The Residence's formal dining room hosted many famous guests from vice presidents to movie stars. Find out who sat where in Chapter 2.

11

The mansions' lower level staircase led to a large-screen TV and billiards table that were a favorite hangout for the Venturas' son Tyrel.

12

Many of the staff of the Governor's Residence paused April 30, 2002, just before we closed the mansion doors for a final group picture with the woman who donated her family home for the state to use in the first place, Mrs. Olivia Dodge (center). From left are: Gardener Bill Suchy, Housekeeper Beth Karlisch, Assistant Residence Manager Cassandra Yarbrough, Steward Theresa Finnegan, Administrative Assistant Sylvia Sanchez, myself (Dan Creed) and Housekeeper Sandy Ellingson.

13

Staff paused mid-work for a quick photo with Miss Minnesota (center). Those pictured are Steward Theresa Finnegan, Assistant Residence Manager Cassandra Yarbrough, myself and Administrative Assistant Sylvia Sanchez.

14 We were one big happy Residence family the day the Venturas affirmed their wedding vows. Pictured in the center are Chefs Nate and Ken Grogg. Others pictured include security and catering staff as well as Housekeeper Sandy Ellingson (center left), Administrative Assistant Sylvia Sanchez (center right), Steward Theresa Finnegan and myself.

15

Assistant Resident Manager Casssandra Yarbrough and Housekeeper Sandy Ellingson had to mix it up more often in the kitchen after budget cuts eliminated a chef position.

16

I'm poised on the Residence terrace in my typical official position, waiting to serve the Governor while he conducts the state's business.

17

My wife Jan often volunteered her time to set up, serve and clean up nonprofit and special events at the Residence. She also made an elaborate Hawaiian-style cake, complete with edible flowers and sparklers, for the Governor's 50th Birthday party.

18

I'm pictured here in the Residence "control room" from which staff launched many a successful event.

19

20

19 & 20. Staff of the Governor's Residence certainly got to see all sides of Governor Jesse Ventura, from leather-jacket clad administrator to the hula-skirted birthday boy.

The Governor was particularly annoyed at the media attention that his decision to close the Residence in spring of 2002 brought. Reporters had filmed the removal of some donated art and loaned furniture the last week the Residence was open. When one reporter asked the Governor about the closing, he called John Wodele and who called me with orders to "clear the house and tell them they can't come back." In effect, all reporters were banned from inside the Residence for the last two days the mansion was officially open. They covered the closing from outside the closed gates.

A few months later, when Governor Ventura left office, he saved a final parting shot for the Minnesota media. "As of Monday, you will fear me," he promised them at his last press conference.

I doubt their notebooks were shaking much. After all, if the mighty giant had already slain himself, why would David fear Goliath's final moan?

Others, though, still had more to fear from the Governor's wrath, staff and myself included.

CHAPTER 7

JESSE: THE VICTIM

Though Jesse Ventura fueled many fires, sometimes the Governor just got burned. Tyrel Ventura probably threw the most kindling his father's way when his personal choices made for sensational news stories. The First Son's judgment was often clouded as the young man searched for fun, friends and fame in his father's shadow.

One choice in friends was particularly damaging. In July 2000, Tyrel invited a new friend from California—an imposter named Stewart Peters—to stay with him at the Residence. The imposter had convinced Tyrel that he was a budding actor, Coleman Hughes, and the brother of *Home Improvement* TV show star Jonathan Taylor Thomas. The Governor and First Lady approved of the invitation and instructed staff to treat Coleman not just as any other guest but as part of the family. Though Ventura spokesman John Wodele would later insist Hughes/Peters lived at the Residence less than two weeks, he actually called the guest bedroom home for nearly a month.

The gregarious young man came to Minnesota under the guise of working with Tyrel on a movie the Ventura son was directing. Coleman was charming and likeable. He loved a good time and wanted you to join in. He was funny and did amusing imitations of people, including the Governor. Everyone was swayed a bit by his personality. I was too, at first, and even played racquetball with Coleman. The Governor was taken with our imposter as well and would occasionally invite Coleman to join him in the family room for a cigar and conversation. (I guess, Jesse Ventura's military training never included enemy identification or interrogation!)

Tyrel's guest no doubt enjoyed his stay. Housekeepers cleaned his room and did his laundry. Staff took phone messages and did computer work when he needed letters written. State police, working as security agents, even gave him occasional rides to places around town. He helped himself to food anytime he wanted and to the liquor cabinet regularly. All in all, the Californian had a nice gig going for him in Minnesota—at tax-payers' expense.

It wasn't long, however, before staff started to suspect there was something underneath Coleman's personable exterior. He was, to be honest, a good actor, but he wasn't that good.

Coleman had a mouth that wouldn't stop telling stories about who he knew and what he'd done. The stories were often enter-taining but eventually got to be so plentiful and outlandish that staff began to suspect he was making much of it up. We had no idea just *how* much!

A few days before his real identity was uncovered, Coleman was telling a whopper to staff in the kitchen. When Sandy final-ly said, "You know, I don't know if I believe you," Coleman got the strangest look on his face.

We knew then that there was something conniving about our guest, and Sandy decided to teach him a little lesson. The next day, Sandy did his laundry per his usual instructions and left it folded neatly on his bed ... with all the flies of all his boxer underwear sewn shut! (We never did see his reaction; he was gone before he even got to wear a pair.)

That same day, an acquaintance of the Venturas, who also knew the actor Jonathan Taylor Thomas, recognized that Coleman was not Thomas' brother. Tyrel himself notified secu-rity. Agents immediately searched the imposter's bedroom and vehicle. In the trunk, they found a tape that showed television news coverage of Coleman pretending to be a budding California hockey star who had just signed a big free agent contract.

A background check revealed Coleman's true identity as Stewart Peters, who impersonated famous people to get a free ride, a free meal or just attention. The gig was up in

Minnesota, however. Tyrel's would-be friend was escorted off the property on Aug. 24, 2000.

Later that week, I tracked down Stewart Peters in California. I felt betrayed and wanted some explanation for the hoax he had played on all of us. "Why did you do this?" I asked. His reply was simple, "Because I could, Dan."

The 22-year-old later explained more to the *Minneapolis Star Tribune's* Randy Furst, after the story broke publicly, in a June 19, 2002, article. Peters expressed no regrets. "If you sneak your way in there, I would recommend it. They had great food. It happened. I would do it again. ... I was basking in the delights of catering staff, and I enjoyed every minute of it."

It goes without saying that the Hughes/Peters incident was a security breach at the Residence. In part because of this experience, security started checking the driver's licenses of anyone unknown coming into the Residence. There were a lot of driver's licenses to check.

LIKE FATHER, LIKE SON

Tyrel had a surprise guest list for Residence security most weekend nights, and many of those guests were people that the Ventura son had met for the first time that night in a restaurant, club or bar.

They would return to the Residence with Tyrel about 2 a.m. and continue the party, drinking and frolicking into the early morning hours. Tyrel would often leave his guests alone in the mansion to go out and get more cigarettes, and security would drive the First Son since he had been drinking.

There were so many people coming in the Residence while the rest of us were home asleep that staff's first question in the morning was usually, "Well, I wonder who is here today."

The majority of the guests Tyrel brought home were women. Some moms would even drive up to the gates in the middle of the night to drop their daughters off, saying the Governor's son had invited them! Some parents actually later confirmed this during a radio interview I did. They called to relate that their daughter met Tyrel at a Denny's restaurant and was immediately invited to the Residence.

Several female guests also stayed overnight in Tyrel's room, the guestroom or, we suspect, the Governor's bedroom.

The Governor's bedroom and other areas of the mansion—such as the Residence offices—were supposed to be off limits. But, several times, staff discovered that visitors had been in those areas as well. A few mornings, for example, we found Residence office computers on with evidence of previously unvisited Internet sites on their servers. More than once, we also found telltale signs that someone had enjoyed a night of passion in the Governor's bed, when the Governor and First Lady were out of town or staying in their Maple Grove home. In addition, the First Lady's nightgown, which hung in the Governor's bedroom, was found hanging in Tyrel's closet one morning, apparently where a female guest had put it after wearing it the night before. I began to wonder if I was manager of the Governor's mansion or the Playboy mansion!

Tyrel knew the house rules and the areas that were off limits to guests. My guess is that, even if he wasn't involved, the First Son often didn't know, or couldn't control, where all his guests were or what they were doing.

As a result, several pieces of Residence furniture were broken during the all-nighters, including an antique barley twist chair. Residence furniture was also stained with food and beer, and three tabletops had to be refinished when cans and bottles left on them created damaging rings in the wood. Actual damages amounted to a few thousand dollars billed to the state. Other costs, including staff cleaning time, were harder to measure.

Public areas of the house were generally left a mess for housekeepers to deal with the next morning. They would often find guests sleeping where they fell, cover partygoers with a blanket and clean around them. If there were events to clean for that day, staff would have to wake the tired teens and send them upstairs or home.

Our housekeepers had to do things for Tyrel that I know they would not have done for their own sons. They picked up women's underclothing that had been tossed in public places and picked up used condoms from the Governor's bed, Tyrel's bed, the bathtub and the bathroom floor. They cleaned up vomit more times than they can count, including in the guestroom where someone puked just a few days after Vice President Al Gore had slept there.

By the spring of 2001, the party situation had reached the

boiling point at the Residence. (The incidents would not gain outside attention until the story erupted in 2002, but more on that later.)

Events climaxed inside the mansion when Jean came in early to clean the lower level for a scheduled morning event. When the housekeeper arrived, Tyrel was upstairs asleep, but two overnight guests were sleeping downstairs on the family room couch and floor. Already frustrated from cleaning up a trashed family room on previous occasions, Jean sternly ushered the men to get upstairs to the family quarters, informing them that an event was scheduled in the room that morning.

The housekeeper later evaluated her comments and thought she may have been too curt with the guests. Worried that she might get into trouble with the Venturas, Jean came to my office to tell me the story. I told her it should be okay but encouraged her to speak to Tyrel about the incident. I felt the matter would be resolved without any other discussion.

The guests had already filled Tyrel in on what happened by the time Jean ran into him. She apologized for her earlier tone and explained that her frustrations that morning stemmed from her need to get into the lower-level family room. Tyrel said everything was okay and he would not tell his mother.

The son did speak to his mother, however, and the First Lady was on the phone to me almost immediately. Terry was blistering mad, not with Tyrel but with the fact that staff had confronted his friends. Terry was so angry that she was unable to listen or to talk earnestly about the matter. Knowing Terry is a very protective mother, I respected her feelings and let her vent.

The next day, the First Lady continued the tirade by sending me a 10-page scathing letter (see page 109) about this incident. Hoping that writing the letter had helped her settle down and wanting to resolve the situation for everyone involved, I called Terry again. The First Lady had a speaking engagement that day, and I arranged for a meeting afterward to review the situation. She and I sat in her driver's state police car in a hotel parking lot for 45 minutes and discussed the details.

It was not the first time I had spoken to Terry about her son's parties and irresponsible behavior. On May 23, 2001, I wrote Terry and Steve Bosacker a memo outlining "issues with Tyrel." I had brought up specific incidents several times in the previous years but gained little parental correction from the Venturas. I do know that Terry would speak with Tyrel most times that I brought up an incident. Those conversations would muffle the party beat for a weekend or so, but the mansion would soon crank up again.

I know of only one occasion when Governor Ventura reprimanded his son about the Residence parties. That occurred in the first months of the administration when the Governor came downstairs early and saw the mess left behind by Tyrel and some friends. The Governor marched upstairs and dragged his son out of bed to clean it up. Staff was elated at the quick response and hoped it was a sign of reactions to come. It was not.

The Governor may have done this more often had he seen the messes for himself. The problem was that the Governor rarely saw the problem because parties were mostly held on weekends when the Governor and First Lady were at their Maple Grove home. When the Governor was "in house," he still didn't see a mess because housekeepers came in at 6 a.m. to clean up the mansion, and the Governor came down between 7 to 8 a.m., long after all was right again in the castle.

Compounding the problem was the fact that the Governor and First Lady seemed to accept, and even defend, Tyrel's behavior as "natural."

The father, who repeatedly told stories about his own wild escapades as a 20-year-old in the Philippines and Las Vegas, seemed to look at Tyrel's activities as a masculine right of passage. Governor Ventura had survived such partying in his youth, and I think he was proud that his son was following in his footsteps.

The Governor's comments to guests often bore that out. At one event, Sylvia overheard the Governor tell a group, "Tyrel should stay here. I told him not to get an apartment when he can stay here and have it made, with the staff doing his laundry, providing him food and taking good care of him. Why wouldn't he stay here?" I also overhead heard him once comment to Dean Barkley, "What other kid can live this comfortably for free?"

The real travesty surrounding the Tyrel incidents was the fact that the Governor, and later many in the media, missed the real story.

Governor Ventura focused on defending his family from being "attacked" by accusations against his son. He said his son's personal life was nobody's business and that Tyrel was a good kid who was doing nothing more than any other normal young adult. In fact, I totally agree that Tyrel's personal life was nobody's business but his, unless his behavior hurt others.

That's where I came in.

The issue was never so much about what Tyrel did, as it was *where* he did it. If these situations took place at the Ventura's Maple Grove home, no one would ever question the events. But, when risky, illegal or irresponsible activities occur inside of the Governor's Mansion, this creates a different situation. Decorum and a healthy respect for state property, and the dignity of the Governor's mansion, must be maintained. As Residence manager, I was charged with that maintenance.

I had seen the mansion threatened by Tyrel's activities so often over the years that I documented and shared my and security's safety concerns with Chief of Staff Steven Bosacker and the First Lady several times. My concern was for the protection of the First Family.

I repeatedly said how worried I was about the security risks of allowing unknown guests, whose backgrounds could not be checked, into the Residence and what those guests might do to, or in, the mansion once inside.

I was also concerned about lawsuits that could result for the Venturas and the state if a drunken partygoer had a car accident after leaving one of Tyrel's parties, especially if that partygoer was underage, as we suspected several were. Ironically, the Governor had signed a 1999 bill that increased the penalty for selling or giving alcohol to someone underage from a gross misdemeanor to a felony if the minor causes death or great bodily harm as a result.

Finally, I was concerned that the state and Governor's reputation were further at risk because of the sexual activity during these parties. If a young person were taken advantage of—even if he or she just claimed to have been taken advantage of—the subsequent investigation and lawsuit could destroy the First Family and damage the state of Minnesota's reputation.

As manager, I was quietly trying from the beginning to protect the Governor and prevent any explosive situations while protecting the mansion, its staff and guests. Because of my concerns, and because of the actual security breach we had with Stewart Peters, security began in the summer of 2001 to check driver's licenses and keep a log of guests arriving late at night.

Sitting in the car that tense morning after the "blow-up," I tried again to convey all this to the First Lady. I stressed that Residence staff liked Tyrel (we really did) and welcomed her son using the Residence to entertain guests. However, staff needed her and Tyrel's support in order to do their work and keep the public areas of the Residence clean and ready for events.

I also emphasized the disrespect for the property shown by some late-night guests and, more seriously, shared with her my concerns regarding possible underage drinking, an accusation based not only on the beer and liquor bottles housekeepers were picking up the mornings after but on security hunches that several guests coming through the gates at night looked younger than 21. We also talked again about how a younger-looking guest had become sick on alcohol and threw up on the guestroom bedspread and in a hat on the night table.

I explained that, to help protect the Venturas and the state, security wanted to have Tyrel's guests leave their driver's licenses at the gate upon entering the Residence. Security would only let a guest leave if the officers (who were all one-time state patrol officers) felt the guest was legally able to drive. Realizing the risk, the First Lady agreed to this plan.

She also asked that I talk with Tyrel about the situation and inform him of the staff's needs. (I am not sure if she talked to her son as well after our conversation.) I welcomed this opportunity and spoke with Tyrel later that day. The meeting went well, and we had fewer problems as a result.

Terry also requested that the housekeeper who confronted Tyrel's guest not be allowed to work on the second floor of the Residence. The First Lady felt this decision would prevent further incidents since the housekeeper wouldn't be running into Tyrel very often. I felt that it was disrespectful thing for Terry to ask because staff was only trying to do the best job they could; however, staff complied with the request. My boss, Chief of Staff Steven Bosacker, sent a note complimenting me on the way the situation was handled.

FRIEND OR FOE?

Family weren't the only relations throwing kindling into the Governor's fire. Ventura friends burned bridges too.

Most problematic from staff's perspective was the First Lady's best friend and official personal assistant, Mari Reed.

The bond this First Lady and her personal assistant shared was unusually tight. Terry Ventura had been friends with Mari for years. They lived in the same neighborhood and had daughters about the same age. They even looked a bit alike, a similarity that seemed to grow the longer Mari worked for Terry. Mari was a model by trade and is slender and attractive like the First Lady. Mari also died her hair black like Terry's. In fact, they were so much alike that guests often thought Mari Reed was Terry's sister, or Terry herself.

Chief of Staff Steven Bosacker was concerned about hiring Mari for the position of First Lady assistant because of her close relationship to the First Lady.

He basically told me to make the final decision about hiring Mari, since she and I would be working in more direct contact. Steven threw the decision at me during my first day on the job. Terry wants her, so you make the call, Dan," he told me. I decided in the First Lady's favor, figuring that since Terry was, at that time, unsure about being First Lady, she would feel more comfortable having someone she already knew and liked in the position.

While this worked well for the First Lady, hiring Mari Reed would prove troublesome to staff.

The problem wasn't just that the First Lady and her assistant were friends but the problem was that Terry trusted—and blindly protected—her friends.

It quickly became common knowledge among both Residence and Capitol staff that Mari was considered not only "untouchable" but "always right."

As the servant to Terry Ventura and the boss to her assistant, I was forever in the middle of an impossible situation. On paper, I was Mari's direct boss, and Steven Bosacker was her ultimate boss. In reality, Mari Reed answered only to Terry Ventura.

Mari never worked on the same playing field as the rest of Residence staff. For example, First Lady assistants historically worked out of the carriage house and were there to assist other staff when they were not busy with First Lady duties. However, Terry arranged for her assistant to have a home office because Mari lived a few blocks from Terry and could be close to the First Lady when she was at the Ventura's Maple Grove home. The well-orchestrated power play placed Mari physically out of the staff loop.

The arrangement only complicated my authority since I was not in a physical position to observe and directly supervise most of Mari's work, as most Residence managers would have been in past administrations. Steven and I discussed, on more than one occasion, that there was no real accountability with Mari as an employee.

Staff often griped to me that they were having to carry some of Mari's load in part because she wasn't in the office as they were and in part because Mari often requested help when she got "swamped," a request she often made with a "my way or the highway" "and now" approach.

Many tasks in Mari's job description were actually completed by other staff, though she got the credit for it. For example, Mari rarely arrived early to set up or stayed to help clean up events. She usually appeared just in time to greet the First Lady and left as soon as Terry did. In addition, nearly all of the hundreds of thank you cards that Mari sent on Terry's behalf (a task clearly spelled out in her job description) were written and sent by Sylvia, under Mari's instructions that they each be done "individually and personally."

Mari considered her real job to be that of official "best friend," and seemed to enjoy taking advantage of the influence and access she had with the First Lady.

Perhaps the first red flag that Mari's standing was higher than the rest of staff in the Venturas' eyes was raised when Mari was a guest at the Jack Nicholson/Sean Penn dinner early in 1999. Terry specifically requested that Mari be included as a guest at the table instead of serving the guests as the rest of staff did that evening. Making the First Lady's assistant a guest, instead of an employee left staff in a "are you one of us or one of them" quandary about Mari's status as their coworker.

The Venturas had invited me over the years to join them as a guest as well. However, I always declined such invitations precisely because I wanted to avoid a "them or us" conflict with my staff. Mari Reed had no such qualms, probably because she assumed that she was really one of "them."

Mari confused dividing lines in December 2001 when she asked if I would volunteer to help her throw a Jade Foundation event at the mansion around Christmas. The foundation, she explained, had no money to pay staff to help with set up and clean up.

I was always willing to pitch in for the foundation that the Venturas founded in their daughter's name. I talked my wife and son into volunteering as well and they accompanied me the Saturday night before Christmas to set up for the charity event.

We were only there a short time when we began to wonder if the event really was a Jade Foundation event. My wife started placing napkins and noticed that each napkin was printed only with a personal name and mentioned to me that it was strange that nothing in the decorations said "Jade Foundation." When the Reeds arrived, they were upset that my son was setting up and told me that they were not paying him. It was a confusing statement because Mari and I already discussed that I, and any other staff, would be volunteering our time to help the foundation.

We volunteers soon took notice that, along with the Governor and Terry Ventura, the only attendees that night were Mari's family, friends and relatives, including her grandmother who had flown in from California. People arrived carrying bottles of wine, gifts were exchanged and a festive atmosphere dominated the room. We began to wonder if Mari was really having a family Christmas at the mansion and we were there to clean up.

When I first started work as Residence manager, Terry and I had drafted usage rules for the mansion, which included the rule that only nonprofit organizations could "rent" the facility. A family Christmas party for a staff member certainly didn't fit those parameters. However, I would have been fine with Mari having the event there if Terry had approved it. After all, though Mari had ordered food from our chefs, she covered the costs and had guests bring drinks so no Residence supplies were consumed. So long as they had been respectful and it didn't get out of hand, staff would have picked up the next day what the family hadn't cleaned up themselves. If Mari had come to me personally and said, "Dan I'm having a personal event and really need help," I probably still would have helped her set up.

What bothered me then, and bothers me still, is that Mari might have used the Jade Foundation name to get me to volunteer my personal time to help her. She did have guests bring checks written out to the Jade Foundation so that the charity appearance was maintained. However, anyone there that night would have assumed, as I did, that this was a private family party.

The party also demonstrated how Mari's relationship with the Venturas earned her special privileges beyond what employees would normally be allowed. Few other Residence employee even thought to ask about having a family party at the mansion.

Whether she meant to or not, Mari portrayed a certain contempt toward the rest of staff. She often wanted the same treatment that the Governor and First Lady were afforded, sometimes even better treatment. For example, on at least two separate occasions Mari Reed demanded that security drive their state patrol escort cars and the Venturas' state vehicle on the shoulder and turn on their flashing lights so that she and First Lady could arrive at a Mall of America movie premiere on time. State police, under-impressed that Mari would be so audacious as to ask them to endanger public safety to accommodate her schedule, repeatedly denied her request. On another occasion, Mari asked the state patrol security officers to call ahead to a movie theater and ask if they could close the venue so that the Venturas, herself and family could attend a premiere in private—a luxury rarely afforded even the biggest movie stars attending their own premieres! The state police refused that request as well.

Mari Reed assumed her influence was a little bigger than it was when she requested complimentary tickets for herself, sister and brother-in-law to a $1,000 a plate charity fundraiser thrown by Sally Pillsbury in 2001. The Governor, who was speaking at the event, purchased tickets for himself and the First Lady out of their own pockets. Naturally, Mari assumed that, as the First Lady's assistant, she would be offered free tickets.

When the charity did not make the offer, Mari asked the state, through Steven Bosacker, to provide her the seats she wanted. Capitol staff ended up getting involved and finally convinced Mari that she would not have free tickets to the event. Ultimately, neither Mari nor anyone from her family attended.

A tight relationship with the First Family didn't always work in Mari's favor, however. After the September 11th tragedies, Mari applied for the opportunity to represent the state of Minnesota at Ground Zero. She was accepted and elated at the chance to be "First Lady." Then, Terry suggested that she and the Governor go along. Mari was furious, storming around the Residence, because she had orchestrated the opportunity, and Terry was waltzing in and stealing her limelight. I felt genuinely bad for her because this had been her one opportunity to shine alone. Now, she had to share it.

The Venturas should have let Mari have her day. The First Couple's visit to Ground Zero did not gain them favorable attention. The Governor granted exclusive coverage of the event to national media and closed the coverage door to Minnesota press. The incident only escalated the war between the Governor and the local media.

Though a fuming Mari told staff that "my relationship with Terry is going to be changing after all of this," Mari was soon back in her post as chief confidant.

Omitting information was one of the most mischievous kinks Mari threw into the communication chain that went from staff through her to the First Lady. It was frustrating to know that Terry was given less than the whole story, or a different story, and misunderstood much of what was going on in the Residence as a result. Communicating with the First Lady became more of a challenge for everyone, including Terry, because Mari was the filter in the middle.

A case in point occurred when the Venturas traveled to Washington, D.C., to attend the National Governors Conference, and Mari accompanied the First Lady on the trip.

When the Governor and First Lady returned from any trip, the chefs would have meals available. Typically, I would call Mari or the security detail traveling with the Venturas to verify the schedule and find out the family's specific food requests. This particular day, we were unable to contact anyone because they were in locations where cell phones were not permitted for most of the day.

Since it was getting late and we had not heard from Washington, the chefs prepared a meal for the Venturas' return.

Just before boarding the plane home, Mari called the office to request dinner for the First Family. Since I was in a meeting at the Capitol, Sylvia took the call. Mari requested three different entrées for the Governor, First Lady and Jade: steak, lobster and chicken.

Normally, different menu requests were not a problem for the chefs but, in this case, the food for the meal had already been purchased and prepared. Sylvia tried to explain the situation to Mari; however, the First Lady's assistant only kept reiterating the requests, saying, "This is what they wanted."

Had I taken the call, I would have asked Mari to let Terry know that the food was already prepared, and I do not believe that Terry would have minded. But, Sylvia couldn't get past Mari.

Consequently, the chefs had to go out shopping again and prepare a new menu.

When I returned from my meeting, I found the entire staff in an angry mood, upset because their work had been wasted and they'd been talked down to by one of their peers.

As far as I know, Terry was never made aware that the chefs had prepared another meal. Terry was also left in the dark as to communications I had with Mari in the last week that the Residence was open, as staff was planning the final event, a dinner with the ambassador from Canada. By that time, the Residence's two chefs were gone, and office staff and housekeepers were filling the gap of preparing meals and special events. The First Lady wanted to add a final luncheon to that day's schedule and had Mari call to make the arrangements. I told Mari honestly that "if given a choice, I'd rather not have the luncheon that day" because of the burden already placed on a limited staff to prepare for the dinner. However, I also said that we would do whatever the First Lady wanted. Instead of communicating most of this to Terry, Mari complained to the First Lady that staff was "being uncooperative" with her. Once again, the First Lady was raking me over the coals for not being nice to Mari.

Miscommunications between Mari and the Governor's staff had become so common that security and other staffers kept logs of their conversations with Mari so that they had something to back up their side of the story.

Staff was also careful about what we said around Mari Reed. We knew that any small slight would be immediately reported to the First Lady and usually reported with whatever words made Mari look the best.

The most damaging example occurred in the last month that the Residence was open. Staff were frustrated because we knew by then that we were losing our jobs, yet Mari was not only keeping her position but had just received a raise. A raise was the direct opposite of what I had proposed when the Venturas first came to me with a need for deep cuts in Residence expenses, including trimming 1.5 staff positions. With a directive from the Governor himself that there were "no sacred cows" and since the First Lady was cutting back on her activities, I sent Terry a memo that suggested combining Mari's position with another position, making the First Lady assistant job part time. Steven Bosacker applauded me for the bold suggestion but cautioned that the idea would never be accepted. The First Lady rejected the idea immediately.

During the last month the Residence was open, Mari arrived at the mansion just before a charity luncheon that the First Lady was hosting was set to begin. She met Sylvia and Theresa standing in the mansion waiting to greet guests. Theresa returned a hug when Mari approached her with one. Sylvia—a passionate and compassionate woman with a hug for everyone from the First Lady to the gardener—didn't feel like hugging Mari, who had approached the women with a syrupy, "Hi, sweeties, how are you?"

Sylvia said "hello" cordially in return but, when Mari hugged her, Sylvia didn't hug the First Lady's assistant back. She left her arms at her sides. Mari left the embrace and walked immediately through the foyer and upstairs to the First Family's quarters where the First Lady was getting ready.

Within minutes—maybe even seconds—the First Lady was charging down the stairs and straight to Sylvia. "Do you have a problem with Mari?' she demanded. "Because she just let me know you were very rude to her." Sylvia insisted, as guests were arriving, that this was not the place to discuss any staff problems and they could talk about it later. Terry then turned her gaze to Theresa and thanked the steward for "being the one person who is nice to Mari."

The next morning, staff got a scathing fax from Terry scolding all of us for how terribly Residence employees treated Mari. I thought Sylvia was going to lose it; she was really upset that just because Sylvia didn't feel like hugging someone *all* staff were reprimanded. I assured Sylvia that it would be okay but, in my heart, I knew differently. This was just the latest example of how Mari's report about staff could alter the First Lady's opinion. For her part, Terry would never believe that a friend could be anything but honest and loyal. The First Lady had blinders on. No matter what anyone said, Mari could never be lying; it had to be staff that wasn't telling the whole truth.

The truth that shone through that day was that Mari had again added fuel to the fire that burned us in the end.

A REPRIMAND FROM TERRY

Terry Ventura sent me the following handwritten note during our ongoing discussions about Tyrel parties at the Residence. I have typed it as she wrote it.

Dan:

As much as I appreciate my staff and all they do for me and my family, I have come to feel a certain uneasiness in my own home here in St. Paul. I feel as though the staff looks on the house as theirs and that we are interlopers. It is up to you as residence manager to maintain the careful balance of respect and deference to the Governor and his family while helping to enhance the type of informal relationship I have allowed to be a perk of working in a state owned facility.

I did not tolerate the abuse and attitude of the chefs or certain members of security and will not allow it in the rest of the staff. I have begun to notice that it is taken for granted, yet again, that Tyrel and his friends are thought of and treated as an imposition and a nuisance in our home. That when Jade and I are here it seems like "one more thing" you all must put up with and there is not as much attention to detail and cleanliness in the care of our rooms and personal belongings. I also notice that my orders are second guessed or incomplete.

With Jade and I at the ranch more, the Governor rarely staying overnight and Ty coming and going, I find it hard to believe that we are so much trouble to the staff.

I was amazed to hear that someone actually ordered Tyrel and his friends out of the lower level family room at 7 a.m. and that they were informed that these are "public rooms!" If there are events to take place mornings the to avoid concerns as to usage, Tyrel should, from now on, have a printed schedule of events put in his room weekly.

The staff seems to have use of the house for private functions at will as I was told not to asked that there is to be a baby shower here for a relative of our staff. Then there was a disappearing nightgown incident where I was told it was hung up in my dressing room so I must have taken it home and that the entire upstairs and laundry room had been searched. But when I walked into Ty's closet, it as the first article of clothing hanging on the rod!

You know that as 1st Lady, I have always tried to thank people, show interest in their personal lives and be as grateful and gracious as I can to all our staff.

I am not perfect but I am also maintaining a staggering amount of responsibility publicly and privately. I am not asking for the world here. Just the respect and courtesy due to me and my family members.

Let it be completely understood that as far as me, my family and friends are concerned, there are no quote "public rooms," in this house and that anyone who thinks they are *above us or are entitled to anything here, they are wrong! I will not tolerate it ever. We are paying for our stay here with real dollars and public service. We all deserve respect and courtesy at all times.*

That being said, you also know that I appreciate and honor hard work and sacrifice. I try to recognize it often and will try to be more diligent in responding to it publicly.

Thank you for all you do and I expect that you will handle this with your usual grace and professionalism and will not share my letter or words with anyone. Just make it so.

Sincerely,
Terry Ventura

| CHAPTER 8 |

JESSE: THE KING

Sometime into his first year, Governor Ventura declared himself King. And, why not? As king, Jesse Ventura could be the Governor he really wanted to be. A king, unlike a governor, can say and do whatever he wants and doesn't have to tolerate the inconvenience of other thoughts. Unlike a governor elected to serve the people, a king serves only himself and enjoys a people and staff who serve him, and his opinions, without question.

Jesse Ventura has always had a royal air about him. He was, and still is, an "I" guy who believes that only what affects him personally is important, that his opinions are always right, and that those who disagree with him are disloyal subjects. Political analyst Wy Spano drove that point home when he noted in Politics in Minnesota that "no other Governor in Minnesota history, in his State of the State (addresses), used the pronoun 'I' as much as Jesse Ventura."

Governor Ventura went so far as to have his own likeness immortalized, not in statues like kings past but in action figures and bobblehead dolls.

His enemies warned Minnesotans that Caesar might not be the "man of the people" we imagined. In his Oct. 11, 1999, Time article after the Playboy comments, Ventura nemesis Garrison Keillor told the world that Minnesota's king "has never confessed to a single regret or second thought and ... struts around St. Paul, a big small town, with a retinue of bodyguards, emitting a great air of celebrity . . ."

Perhaps Residence staff should have seen the kingdom coming long before we realized we were serving it. But the truth is we never believed, never wanted to believe, that most of the Governor's pomp and circumstance was any more than a wrestling personality farce played out for public entertainment and political appeal. We never thought he could, or would, hold court in private. Like most of Minnesota, we staff thought the Governor was just trying to be funny, at first.

The truth behind his humor slowly and painfully revealed itself to all of us.

From the beginning of his term, the Governor had joked to guests and the media about how great it was to live in a mansion "where staff waited on you."

Even before he moved into the mansion, he told *City Pages* (December 1998) how much he liked his new job as Governor because, "I can walk around now and say, 'Jump!' and there are four people who say, 'how high?'" (My guess was those four people were eventually myself, Theresa, Sylvia and Sandy).

He was hardly at the Residence a month when Governor Ventura relayed to *Newsweek* Feb. 15, 1999, how much he enjoyed being waited on at the mansion. "I plop myself down in the chair, the food comes, and then I can go plop myself down in front of the TV. I don't have to stack the dishwasher. They do it."

One day, the Governor just came right out and said it.

"It's great to be king!" he exclaimed to *Playboy* in that ill-fated article, and many times since on national television. "The best thing is there's no one in the state who can tell me what to do."

A NEW 'ATTITUDE'

The transformation of Governor Ventura and family from grateful, unexpected guests at the mansion into demanding tenants, who'd come to expect even the smallest of conveniences, began in their first months at the Residence.

We staff were not blameless in this attitude change. We all enjoyed doing extra things for the family. Though the Governor rarely expressed it, Terry especially seemed appreciative in the beginning and said so often. She was quick to compliment and would write us thank you notes for a job well done. Terry asked us if we minded doing this or that and expressed her gratitude personally when we'd gone the extra mile.

Terry even told *Newsweek* in a February 1999 article that the staff "feel like they're part of my family now." Staff felt the same way about the Venturas. However, I know now that I should have paid more attention to a warning we got at a National Governor's Residence Managers Conference: "No matter how close you feel, you'll never be in that family Christmas photo."

Still, we believed the Venturas liked and respected us, and that made it easy for us to want to do personal things for the family. It was our duty to make the Governor and Mrs. Ventura look good to their guests and extend their and the state's hospitality to every visitor, but we were all willing to go above and beyond in our jobs to help them, especially Terry.

When the First Lady asked for a favor, staff gladly pitched in, often after hours, on our own time, without pay. Many times, I would take food our chefs had prepared out to the Venturas' Maple Grove ranch—and one time to Terry's mother's house—on my way home from work. The staff and I also volunteered extra hours to help with family events such as birthday parties for the children. In addition, if I knew the Venturas were having a private event at the Residence over the weekend, I would stop in to check on things or come in on Sundays to clean up. The Sunday after the Governor's birthday party at the Residence was especially grueling. It took me all day to get the mansion back in shape.

In time, however, doing these favors became more of an expectation than an extra. Like anyone, I suppose, the Venturas got used to having someone cook and clean for them and soon took it for granted. As the Venturas, of course, the family almost naturally took "for granted" to another level.

The Governor would often say that he was the captain of our ship, and we all knew to "salute" him. The First Lady insisted from our first moments together that staff always call her "Terry." The Governor made no such informal gestures, however. We were to call him "Governor," never "Jesse." Even his wife called him "Governor" much of the time. The family did like things neat, especially Terry. For the most part, though, they just didn't want to be bothered with doing the "neat-making" themselves.

Tyrel was especially messy, even for a teenage boy. To this day, I don't think I can tell you what color the carpeting was in his bedroom. I often felt that the Governor should have declared his son's room a disaster area, but he never saw a problem with it. Staff learned, in time, to give up on the room and, like many a parental guardian, just shut the door when visitors came.

The whole family eventually developed the same laissez-faire attitude toward their own filth. Towels soaked where they dropped on the bathroom floor, dirty clothes slung far from the hamper, and dropped food worked its way into carpets and upholstery until staff came by to whisk it away.

A case in point happened the day we bid farewell to Vice President Gore at the airport. I didn't stay for the full Air Force Two tour because I had to check on preparations for a picnic that night. The chefs had prepared food early and put it in coolers but, when I arrived, I discovered that Tyrel and some friends had gotten into the coolers and eaten some of the food. They'd also gone into the pantry and knocked a bottle of cherries off the shelf. Most disrespectfully, they'd left the oozing cherry juice and glass on the floor for someone—me—to clean up.

I wasn't as upset with Tyrel as some might think. After all, I knew that those cherries did not fall very far from the tree. Disrespect is taught, and when it came to having the expectations of the ruling class, the Governor was a great teacher. The best example I can give revolves around the mansion haunting story that the Governor loved to tell, though he never related staff's part in it.

The Governor was home late one Friday night when our Resident ghost Elizabeth upset dishes on a pantry shelf, and they crashed to the floor. The Governor heard the crash and came in and saw the dishes on the floor. He called Terry to tell her about it. Terry called me at home early Saturday morning not only to relay the story but also to tell me that I needed to come in and clean up the "big mess" that the ghost had left. I live in Elk River, Minn., 40 minutes away and made the trip daily to the mansion without complaint. However, my wife and I were none-too-happy when we both made a cross-town drive that morning and I arrived to find only a couple of broken saucers on the floor. The Governor could have picked it up himself in 30 seconds and put the pieces in a nearby garbage can.

But, he never would have thought to do so.

The real rub of this story came a little later when the Governor was sharing the tale on local radio and commenting on how he was alone in the Residence because, "you know state workers are out the door at 5."

What an absolute kick in the gut thing to say! I got quite hot under the collar listening to him berate the very state workers who were never out the door at 5 (unless he meant 5 a.m.). The Governor knew full well that his staff gladly stayed well past 5 p.m. most nights—*without* overtime pay—to serve him, his guests and the state of Minnesota. We even came in on Saturday mornings, at the Venturas' beck and call, to pick up the dirt that was forever beneath them.

ROYAL MOVES

Perhaps because she knew what slobs her boys could be, Terry was especially demanding on staff where cleaning was concerned. She always wanted the house perfect and grew into more of a perfectionist as time went on.

It was mostly Terry who would confront staff when things were out of order, and she was particular about items being moved on the dresser, especially if the Governor's cigar box had been moved. Housekeepers went to great pains to be sure that if they picked something up to dust, they put it right back in the same place.

Terry was most upset when she thought staff had moved something and would often directly accuse us when an item was missing. Several times, the Governor would forget where he left his golf clubs and staff would be blamed for moving them. Usually, security would find them in the back of his car.

Terry got quite upset the day she thought that the housekeepers had moved her nightgown. We later found it in Tyrel's closet and returned it (without questions, though we had many) to the Governor's bedroom.

She was really fuming the day the Governor couldn't find his goggles. The way she was barking orders and accusations you would have thought we'd absconded with his pink boa! Terry even got on the Residence intercom and screeched that whoever had moved them should return them to the Governor "immediately!" I was especially embarrassed because that was Sandy's first day on the job and Terry had come across so demeaning. "They're not usually this bad," I tried to convince her.

The few times we did feel the Governor's wrath over seemingly tiny household matters were even more unpleasant. He had a way of addressing a wrongdoing as if you should drop and give him 20.

The Governor was only particular about how we handled his most treasured items, such as his workout clothes and Speedo swimming suit. The care and handling of his beloved cigars demanded extra special attention, however, as Jean painfully learned in our first weeks together.

After coming in to help with a family event, Jean was tidying up the foyer and noticed a little butt of cigar in an ashtray, left over from the Governor's puffing the evening before. She cleaned out the butt and ashes and threw it away in the kitchen. Then, she felt the chill of a gubernatorial presence behind her. "Don't you every touch my cigars again!" he growled, admonishing her that no matter how little a stub was left, she was to leave the cigar remnants right where they were.

Another day soon after, Sandy carried the Governor's laundry upstairs to put it away. She couldn't help but notice how messy the Governor's dresser drawers were getting, noting that, unless she had the brawn of a Navy SEAL, she couldn't even pull a drawer out to put a clean t-shirt in. As a little extra, Sandy cleaned and straightened the drawers for the Governor.

His clothes were so tidy that the Governor couldn't find a particular t-shirt. Sandy had unknowingly broken two rules. She "hid" the Governor's favorite things and moved something Terry didn't want moved. The First Couple blew their cool and decreed that from that day hence staff was only to stack the Governor's clean clothes on a stool in the bedroom. They were never to put any of the Governor's things away in the bedroom again. Furthermore, staff was ordered to always keep the Governor's favorite clothes on the top of that stack. Regardless of how much rearranging it would take, the housekeepers knew to keep moving his Navy SEAL t-shirts and workout gear to the top.

Our emperor, after all, had many favorite robes; he just wore no underwear.

Well, at least that's what Jesse Ventura told people. Sandy, Jean and Beth all swear that they spent a great deal of time washing the royal undergarments, even before an underwear manufacturer—learning of the Governor's carefree preferences—sent him a huge supply to try on for size. When the boxes arrived, the housekeepers confirmed that they weren't sure if the Governor needed them. For all the washing they'd done, the ladies were convinced that the Governor—or someone—in that mansion had been wearing the gubernatorial briefs all along.

EVERYONE FOR GRANTED

Though the Governor and First Lady hinted at royal expectations from in the beginning, it was son Tyrel who actually expressed it first.

While on a radio talk show in early 1999, Tyrel inadvertently referred to the mansion housekeepers as servants. Terry Ventura was furious, then, at the statement, and staff were relieved and appreciative when she made her son immediately apologize in person and on the air to the housekeepers. However, as the Ventura term wore on, I think everyone in the family, even Terry, began to take a more "servants" attitude toward staff.

The Venturas seemed to consider less and less how their decisions, or indecisions, would affect staff. So long as their needs were met, all was right in the kingdom. For example, the Venturas did a lot of last-minute schedule and menu changes, which had staff hopping at, and back to, the mansion to accommodate them. Though some changes are the nature of a Governor's schedule, the Venturas seemed to like to fly by the seat of their pants depending on what was going on politically.

Our chefs and staff often stayed late to ensure a delayed meal was kept warm and tasty for hours after it was supposed to be served. Staff had few complaints when delays were due to official state business. However, delays in the Ventura Residence were more often created to accommodate unexpected guests, watch a favorite TV show or fit in a last-minute workout that the Governor suddenly added to his own agenda.

The Venturas' event schedules also seemed to change with their moods. If either got wind of something that wasn't right or thought someone would be present they didn't want there, they'd change the venue of an event—like a king and queen rushing back over the drawbridge to safe haven.

Terry would even cancel an event we were preparing for, or preparing her for, if she felt she'd be uncomfortable or thought that there might be a scene. She most often avoided political events and events attended by many legislators. There were many times that Capitol staff wanted Terry to appear but she chose not to, such as at lunch for the Crown Prince of Norway and dinner for the Canadian Ambassador. When she felt Capitol staff had scheduled too many things on her schedule, Terry could get that "someone moved something" tone in a hurry.

Much of these last minute inconveniences and special requests are part of any gubernatorial household, but many of the Venturas' demands reached beyond normal. Theresa and I were the staff most often called away from the mansion to the Governor's Maple Grove home to help out with events there. Terry would call on Friday and say, "We're having guests this weekend in Maple Grove and need food." At the snap of her fingers, our chefs baked snacks and meals, and staff would rush to get ready so that I could drive the food out there after work.

If Terry wanted help with something specific at the ranch, she'd often call Theresa to handle it. Theresa was at the ranch a lot and was often called on to help the First Lady with personal tasks. For example, it was Theresa who enjoyed an afternoon decorating the Governor's bedroom for Valentine's Day with rose petals, candles and balloons at Terry's special request.

Sometimes, the Venturas took requests even further and called us away from our own homes to help them with something "important." For example, one Thanksgiving Day, Theresa left her family dinner to come to the mansion because the Venturas couldn't find some things in the kitchen.

At the time, Theresa, the rest of staff, and myself rarely minded even such personal intrusions. Staff truly believed that we were serving the state by serving the Venturas and saw these extra errands as a part of that higher purpose. We worked tirelessly to make the Governor look the part of a good statesman and to make his kingdom shine in the eyes of others. We were proud of the role we played in his success.

Looking back now that so much water has fallen over the Residence dam, staff see such incidents without the rose-colored glasses we once wore. We realize now how often the Venturas took advantage of our service and our loyalty.

A ROYAL EXAMPLE

Jesse Ventura's shortcomings as the King of Minnesota became especially glaring to my wife and I after we visited the home of a real "king of the people" in October 1999, when we traveled to the nation of Jordan for a conference.

Knowing that Jordan's King Hussein had visited the Mayo Clinic in Minnesota during the illness before his death, I asked Minnesota Chief of Staff Steven Bosacker if he would like me to hand deliver a message from the Governor to the Queen of Jordan. The Governor liked the idea as well and sent a note to Queen Noir, inviting her to visit the Governor's Residence the next time she was in Minnesota. My wife and I were invited to the palace to deliver the note to the Queen's chief of staff.

At the royal palace, we learned the story of the reign of King Hussein. Jordan's governor was a real King of the People who would occasionally disguise himself as a taxi cab driver, pick up riders and engage them in conversations about what they really thought about their king's latest plans. The king knew that his advisors would always tell him he was right, expecting that would be what a king would want to hear from his servants. But King Hussein knew, respected and accepted the truth. Not only was he sometimes wrong but, as king, he genuinely wanted to know what his people thought about the job he was doing for them.

Another fascinating true story I learned about King Hussein involved his personal chef. Enemies of the king had paid the chef money to poison Hussein. The chef was thrown into prison and condemned to hang for his crime. One day, when the king was driving into the palace compound, he saw the chef's wife and children holding a vigil on behalf of the condemned man. The king was so moved that he invited the chef and his family to lunch.

Reluctantly, the chef ate lunch thinking that the king was trying to get revenge by poisoning the chef's whole family. The king said he had other ways of getting revenge and told the man to go home for one week with his family and then come back to work. The chef remained a loyal servant for the rest of the king's life.

The contrast between that king and my king back home in Minnesota was bigger than the distance between their two castles. Governor Ventura prided himself on his vengeful nature and his ability to force people to see things his way. "My rules or the highway," a play on the famous phrase, was one of his oft-quoted quips.

Governor Ventura would never think to vanquish an enemy, real or imagined, through compassion and forgiveness as King Hussein had done. If King Hussein was a royal yardstick by which a would-be king could be measured then, I realized, Minnesota's giant wrestler was at least one yard short.

| CHAPTER 9 |

JESSE: THE POLITICAL SPOILER

J ust as the Governor was no king, I am no political pundit or commentator. In fact, I specifically tried to ignore political issues while I was Residence manager so that I could more objectively serve the Governor and the state. However, it's important that readers learn something of the war games that went on between the Legislature and Governor Ventura in order to better understand how Residence staff got caught in the crossfire.

For all the blustering the Governor did at home and in public, he probably most enjoyed wielding a little royal wrath in political circles.

His love of a good fight, quick temper, vindictive nature and unsympathetic ear did little to win him friends at the state Capitol.

But, then, Governor Ventura had enough problems just getting along with his own party. To this day, some within the former Reform Party believe Governor Ventura's abrasive style, political and personal choices, and controversies led to the destruction of the party and damaged the credibility of independent parties for a long time to come.

When he was elected Governor, many thought Ventura was the new king of a blossoming political movement in America, a movement to find a consensus in the center for independent candidates' supporters. Ross Perot's United We Stand presidential election groundswell in 1992 gave breath to the Reform Party. Reformers later found rebirth and national inspiration in Ventura's underdog election as Governor. They believed that Governor Ventura's personality was big enough to carry the Reform Party message not only nationally but also into the mainstream.

"His election gave minor parties new energy and publicity," noted Tom Squitieri in a June 20, 2002, *USA Today* article. "Ventura's success at building a coalition of young people, first-time voters and those who are fiscally conservative but socially liberal was seen as the blueprint for the minor-party candidates."

In the beginning, the Governor seemed to be bringing the independent-led coalition and platform together in Minnesota. To much public acclaim, he appointed a bipartisan (even tri-partisan) cabinet and made good on his promises to make Government give something back to the people. He issued tax rebates and put through a budget that largely held spending in check.

Former Congressman and Democrat Tim Penny, an unpaid Ventura advisor who later became an independent gubernatorial candidate, was as excited as anyone about the possibilities. Unlike Ross Perot, Ventura had done "much to move Reform beyond personality and to substance," Penny wrote in a Sept. 23, 1999, *Christian Science Monitor* column.

The Governor used his national attention to raise awareness of third party candidates elsewhere as well. He traveled to some fund-raisers where he signed autographs to help raise political donations and/or endorsed Reform Party and Independent candidates such as Wisconsin Libertarian candidate for governor Ed Thompson and New Jersey Independent candidate for governor William Schluter.

Governor Ventura began as the case study for how other third party candidates could rise between the debris of traditional parties and succeed. However, the Governor became the blueprint for how to squander political opportunity.

For a few Reform Party voters, questions began with 1998 rumors that then candidate Jesse Ventura had convinced—and some charge bribed—Reform Party candidate Bill Dahn to switch to the Republican Party ticket when Ventura election staffer, Dean Barkley, paid the man's $600 re-registration fee after a meeting with Dahn in his St. Paul home. With no primary challenger, Ventura could focus his efforts and funds on the main gubernatorial race. Ventura all but admitted to the implication on Joe Soucheray's radio show in July 1998, when he said, "What if we did do that? What's the big deal about that?" Most party members, like many Minnesotans and myself included, were too caught up in Ventura's charisma and political promise to give such allegations much attention at the time.

When Governor Ventura spoke, Reformers listened. After he was elected, Minnesota's new independent Governor gave Jack Gargan a soft endorsement for party chairman at the National Reform Party Convention in 1999. Conventioneers loyally voted Gargan into office, despite the fact that the Governor made the endorsement by speakerphone because he was home in Minnesota nursing a sore back.

Hints of personality clashes ahead were cast at the convention, however, when past Reform Party favorite Ross Perot failed to even mention Governor Ventura in his speech. The Governor made it quite well known that he held little affection for Perot, especially because the Reform Party founder had ignored the Ventura campaign completely. Governor Ventura always held a grudge against Perot for failing to consider him a candidate worthy of campaign donations. According to a Feb. 21, 2000, *Time* magazine, the two Reform Party leaders had actually spoken only twice.

It was Ventura's General Patton versus Perot's General Montgomery, except that in the late 20th Century, the Reform Party didn't have a centralist General Eisenhower to keep the two prima donnas from showing up each other in battle instead of fighting the real war.

By 1999, Ross Perot was reportedly growing tired of yielding the spotlight to Ventura and tried to steer the party back toward him by denying Gargan and Governor Ventura access to party membership lists. This decision infuriated the Governor. The slight also upset one of the Governor's chief advisors and campaign manager Dean Barkley, who had been one of the Reform Party founders, along with Perot, and had twice run as a Reform Party candidate for U.S. Senate and paved the independent political way for Jesse Ventura.

When Perot fired such a warning shot across the Ventura bow, he had to know that war would be imminent. Governor Ventura fired back on Feb. 11, 2000, by abandoning the Reform Party barge all together.

The Governor knew such an announcement would be controversial and changed the planned press conference site several times. The press conference was eventually scheduled for inside the Governor's Residence (where an interview with ABC newsman Sam Donaldson was later conducted). Staff rushed to make last minute changes, and we were still getting everything in place as local and national press arrived. There was simply too much media interest, and even the mansion couldn't hold all the reporters.

Though it was a particularly cold day in Minnesota, we had no choice but to hold the event outside. The Governor made his announcement from the front steps of the Residence while wearing his Rolling Stones jacket. It was so cold that I could actually see the frustration in his breath as Governor Ventura exhaled.

Officially, the Governor told his audience, he was leaving the Reform Party because it was pulling itself apart instead of pulling together. The party, he said, was "hopelessly dysfunctional," accomplishing nothing with all the infighting. It had become "unworthy" of the American people's support.

More importantly to Governor Ventura, the party had become unworthy of him. "The national Reform Party did virtually nothing, zero, to get me elected," the Governor stressed, as he reiterated the many things he had done to bolster the party and independent movements.

I believe the Governor was sincere in his reasons, but I also quietly wondered that day if all the pre-decision bluster heard around the Residence—about Perot and a small group within the party trying to overthrow the Governor's ally Jack Gargan—also had something to do with the announcement.

Governor Ventura's decision to leave the party had immediate and lasting ramifications. As a result, and at his encouragement, the Minnesota Reform Party recreated itself as the Minnesota Independence Party.

More significantly, the Ventura departure threw the National Reform Party Convention into a near-riot in Tennessee the next day. Conventioneers voted Gargan out as chairman, and Ventura-supported presidential hopeful Donald Trump withdrew his name from the race. The party instead gave the presidential nomination to controversial conservative Pat Buchanan. In short time, the Reform Party imploded.

The Reform Party "failed because it was formed the wrong way; it was built around one person, Ross Perot," the Governor later explained in his book *Do I Stand Alone?* "Parties and ideas they stand for shouldn't be dictated by any single personality," he added.

That Ventura ideal wouldn't preclude Minnesota's biggest personality from taking charge, however. For several years, the Governor hinted publicly and privately that he had independent political ambitions beyond the Minnesota governor's office.

"I still believe strongly that I could walk in and steal (the presidential) election at the 11th hour," he told *Newsweek* June 5, 2000. Knowing Governor Ventura as I did, I'm convinced that he not only believed he could do that but secretly wanted to back then.

However, by 2001, even the Governor recognized that he had worked himself out of any further political ambitions and announced that he would not seek re-election to the Governor's office. The national independent parties' leaders were crushed. Without a personality like Ventura to draw attention to the movement, those leaders feared that money and recognition would be harder to raise for their candidates. To his credit, this has not proven entirely true as the now-former Governor does still speak in support of independent parties' candidates and continues as a member of Minnesota's Independence Party.

In the end, however, Governor Ventura did more to split a national third party than he did to unify third party voters. And, he alienated himself from most of the voters who'd elected him.

"The idea of a third party renaissance is now a national joke, courtesy of Ventura," lamented one letter writer in a Jan. 3, 2003, *St. Paul Pioneer Press* article by Jim Ragsdale.

A MAN WITHOUT A PARTY

The Governor did even more to alienate himself from traditional political parties, especially in Minnesota. Some might say that getting under the skin of old-school politicians was the Governor's main motivation.

In many ways, it had to be. As an independent and a political outsider, Governor Ventura was in a nearly no-win situation in the Minnesota Capitol. The Governor didn't have any friends, and he was determined not to make any.

(Friendship) "is essentially what's wrong with politics today," he told Dane Smith of the *Minneapolis Star Tribune* Dec. 1, 2002. "All this nonsense about creating coalitions, you know, snuggling up to everybody, that's just an excuse."

During his first year in office, we hosted a legislative breakfast for the legislators of each political party with the idea that the Governor would spend time with and get to know the senators and representatives he would be working with. When I later asked him if we should do the same thing next year, the answer was an emphatic "no." Steve Bosacker elaborated that the Governor did not want to get to know them better.

The Governor had little tolerance for the debate and deals it takes to make legislation happen either, he told *Newsweek's* Matt Bai early in his administration when the reporter followed the Governor for a day. After listening to lawmakers debate a bond issue for a few minutes, the Governor got up and left, telling Bai, "I can't stand all the rigmarole and posturing. I just had to leave. You know why? Every one of them just wants to be governor."

Though such actions won him few real legislative pals, everyone got along all right at the Capitol during Governor Ventura's first year. This had more to do with popularity than personality. Other politicians knew that the people—the voters—liked the Governor, so they acquiesced to give him some of what he promised. The Governor had the people's taxpayer agenda and made many of his ideas work. He got the "Jesse Bucks" tax rebates he promised, and his first budget passed largely unscathed.

The honeymoon was growing stale by late 1999, however, and Governor Ventura encountered more and more opposition and political game playing in the way of his ideas. Many politicians did, in fact, try to undermine Governor Ventura's efforts simply because he was never one of them and didn't want to play their game their way. "Traditional political powerhouses have been doing everything they can to throw me out of power," the Governor explained in his book *Do I Stand Alone?* "These two blood enemies will try to tear the outsider apart."

One example that I know particularly got under the Governor's skin was the way that Republican lawmakers told the Governor they would support his final budget so long as he didn't make cuts in state funding to cities. After that year's elections were over and the Legislature had rejected most of the

Governor's proposals, the Republicans introduced their own budget fix. Cutting state money to cities was one of biggest solutions proposed.

The natural tension between the traditional parties and a political outsider only intensified as the Governor's frustration brought his personality more and more into the fray.

The combination was so threatening to lawmakers that, without trying to, the Governor achieved the one thing that voters of any state had always thought impossible. He got Democrats and Republicans to agree on something—they agreed that they hated him.

Many politicians disagreed with Ventura every chance they got to the point that even the Governor's good ideas hardly got consideration.

Of course, Governor Ventura did little that would make any one, let alone a political enemy, want to consider anything he had to offer.

Jesse Ventura hates disloyalty and often defines disloyalty as anyone who disagrees *with* him. Nearly every legislator disagreed with Governor Ventura. Because the political parties wouldn't fight with him, Governor Ventura went to war against them with his oft-repeated battle cry, "politics is not violence, but it's still war!"

The political war in Minnesota evolved into a vintage Ventura-style battle where gouging, backstabbing and raucous threats were allowed, even encouraged. In the end, it was Residence staff who became political road-kill.

POLITICAL WAR GAMES

Governor Ventura spent a great deal of time and energy trying to make the Legislature bow before him.

He particularly liked to play games with his political subjects. The classic example was the day he dodged a 1999 bill signing. He had been expected in his office to sign a bill, but when legislators arrived, his doors were locked and he was nowhere to be found. About that same time, I received a warning call at the Residence from Terry, telling me not to tell anyone where the Governor was. The truth is, I didn't know where he was, so I had no problem saying that. I must confess I could have made a pretty educated guess as to his whereabouts.

Governor Ventura loved the fact that everyone, especially traditional politicians, had to drop what they were doing to focus on him for a while. If the Governor couldn't turn legislative heads, he would humiliate, intimidate and retaliate. Legislators often returned the favor in an escalating war of words and inaction that culminated in the transformation of Minnesota from a state with a $3 billion-plus surplus and reserves to a state with a $4.6 billion budget deficit in four years.

The battles were many, but I'll just relay a few.

There were hints of gubernatorial personality and policy conflicts early in the Ventura administration. For example, Governor Ventura ranted around the mansion when he read a 1999 column by Senator Dean Johnson that questioned the Governor's travels to New York City to appear on the *Late Night With David Letterman* show, among other things. He soon called the Senator into his Capitol office chambers for a private scolding of the Senator's public criticism. "Senator, you threw a brick through my window," the Governor charged, according to an interview Johnson gave March 2, 1999, in the *Minneapolis Star Tribune*.

The Senator challenged back, asking the Governor about his "me agenda," whereby Governor Ventura approved only of bills and ideas that matched his views and/or would benefit him. The Governor responded that, "if it impacts me, it impacts other Minnesotans."

After the scolding, Johnson joked with reporters that it was "nice to be up, walking around and healthy." The comment only angered the Governor more because Jesse Ventura always felt that private conversations should stay that way, even between public officials. His view was that virtually anything he said or did was nobody's business but his own.

Legislative animosities were boiling publicly by early 2000 when Representative Greg Davids called Jesse Ventura a "moron" in a January 2000 interview and then refused to apologize. In a statement Davids sent to WCCO's *Facts & Snacks With Legislators* radio show, the Republican representative responded that to appease the Governor's request, "I'd have to apologize first to all the morons."

Perhaps because of their already caustic relationship, the Governor sidestepped Davids for a commissioner appointment early that year. Instead of finding a new commissioner to appoint when Commerce Department Commissioner David Jennings resigned his post, the Governor issued an executive order to merge the Commerce and Public Service departments. He then appointed Public Service Department Commissioner Steve Minn to run the combined department. Governor Ventura not only made the move without consulting the Legislature, he ignored Jennings' own recommendation for his replacement, Representative Davids.

In return, Davids, who was chair of the House Commerce Committee, led a legislative charge to undo the Governor's executive order and reverse the consolidation. The representative also gained the support of other powerful lawmakers, including Senator Steve Novak, chair of the Senate's Jobs, Energy and Community Development Committee. Novak's arguments with the Governor over this and many subjects escalated beyond Capitol walls when the Democrat reportedly heckled the Governor during a business speech.

Meanwhile, Minn and the Ventura camp launched a public relations campaign to garner support for Minn's appointment. That too proved controversial when several of those asked to give support were businesses and utilities that Minn would be charged with regulating.

Minn told the press he believed he was being used as a pawn in a war between the Senate and the Governor. As they always do, the political pawn lost the most in the end.

The Senate overwhelmingly voted against confirming Minn's appointment, the first time in 25 years that the Minnesota Senate had rejected a gubernatorial cabinet nominee.

Governor Ventura accused the Senate of denying the appointment as a personal vendetta against him, just as legislators had accused the Governor of merging the departments out of spite in the first place.

The war only escalated from there. The Governor often muttered something about "self-serving leaches" after he returned to the Residence from the Capitol each day.

As Democrats run against Republicans and Republicans run against Democrats, Ventura's strategy was to run against both, in essence against the entire Legislature. The Governor's hardest political swings were aimed at legislators themselves. For example, Governor Ventura wanted Minnesota to switch to a unicameral government system with one legislative house instead of two, eliminating many political careers. His idea to merge the House and Senate would reduce the number of legislators to 135 and save the state an estimated $25 million per year, he said.

Other Minnesota governors had proposed the unicameral system in the past but not as strongly and as often as Governor Ventura did, stumping for it throughout his election and in his first State of the State address Aug. 17, 1999. The Governor even toured the state of Minnesota in 1999 to promote a 2000 vote for a constitutional amendment to change to a unicameral system.

The unicameral concept seemed fairly popular with voters. Most lawmakers were less enthused about merging both houses and/or about the prospect that nearly 100 of them would lose their political jobs in the process. As I watched the heated debates unfold, I wondered which Governor Ventura liked more: the merits of a unicameral system or the merits of upsetting lawmakers by proposing it.

The Governor did have some lawmakers on his side, however. House Speaker Steve Sviggum supported a bill to bring the unicameral idea to Minnesota voters in the fall of 2000, but the House shot down the measure 76-54 in a May 2000 vote. (A majority vote by each legislative house would have been needed put the unicameral idea on a statewide ballot.) The bill was referred to the House Ways and Means Committee, which was chaired by Representative Dave Bishop, who had formed and served on a legislative steering committee called OUCH (Opponents of a Unicameral House).

The referral essentially killed the idea, and Governor Ventura blamed the politicians for worrying more about their own jobs than the state. Legislators shot back that if the subject meant so much to the Governor, the state's leader should not have been away in Washington, D.C., when the Legislature was debating the unicameral bill.

It was the beginning of a downward spiral in legislative-gubernatorial relations. For his part, the Governor liked to veto much of what the Legislature sent his way. In 2001, for example, Governor Ventura vetoed 16 items from various spending bills using his line-item veto powers. By the last year of his term,

Governor Ventura was the hands-down most overridden Governor in Minnesota history. He was the second Governor to have at least two vetoes overridden in the same year and, in the end, the Legislature overrode him at least nine times. Despite all his Navy SEAL training, Governor Ventura was losing the war in the political trenches.

WELLSTONE: A FINAL INSULT

Perhaps Governor Ventura's most damning political temper tantrum occurred less than two weeks after the unexpected death of well-known U.S. Senator Paul Wellstone, a long-revered Minnesota liberal.

The day before Wellstone's replacement was to be elected, and after the Governor had promised Minnesotans that he would appoint the victor to serve the remaining months of Wellstone's senate term, an angry Governor Ventura suddenly appeared on the Capitol steps and announced the appointment of his advisor and campaign manager Dean Barkley to the vacant senate seat.

The shock of this announcement was largely based on the Governor's tasteless timing and on his apparent about-face concerning the Wellstone appointment

At a press conference hours after the Senator's tragic Oct. 25, 2002, plane crash, Governor Ventura had seemed respectful and gubernatorial in the situation. He ordered the state flags to fly at half-mast through the election and told the press, "I had tremendous respect for Paul, and I will forever be indebted to him for his service and his ultimate sacrifice for this great democracy." The Governor talked about how much he especially appreciated all the Senator had done to support veterans and how the Senator and he would see each other at the veteran's home every Veteran's Day.

Governor Ventura also addressed the fact that he needed to appoint someone to complete Wellstone's term and promised that he would not appoint himself. He later announced that he would wait for the election in a few days and appoint the election winner—either Democrat Walter Mondale or Republican Norm Coleman—to fill the remaining months.

Then, on Nov. 4, 2002, Mondale and Coleman were set for a nationally televised debate that did not include the Governor or any third party candidates. Governor Ventura was furious about the omission and charged that legislators and the media were conspiring against him and third party candidates.

The Governor called a press conference about the debate just as the event was about to begin. As I watched on my television at home, Governor Ventura began ranting about everything from the alleged political conspiracy to how the media was reporting his golf scores. The Governor's anger was quite obvious, so much so that the national cable channel carrying the press conference split the screen to show the debate and lessen the impact of the Governor's tirade on viewers.

Just then, Governor Ventura made his shocking appointment announcement.

Public and legislative outcry was fierce. Few doubted that Barkley, a two-time Reform Party candidate for U.S. Senate who had a good showing in Minnesota, was qualified to carry out the post. They were upset, however, that the Governor had seemingly made the appointment out of spite, especially after he'd promised to appoint the election winner the next day. Many also thought the Governor was "taking care of his friends" by finally giving Barkley the U.S. Senator title he ran for twice.

Tim Penny, the Independence Party gubernatorial hopeful running to replace the Governor (after Governor Ventura bowed out of a second term), had a rally scheduled with the Governor at the Capitol later in the day. Upon hearing the ire of the Governor's speech and appointment, Penny canceled the rally.

I may have been the only Minnesotan not truly shocked by the Governor's vindictive actions. After all, I'd felt the wrath of his temper just a few months before, when the Governor chose to close the mansion and fire Residence staff in order to get back at a Legislature he felt was picking on him.

CHAPTER 10

JESSE: THE BETRAYOR

O n New Year's Day 2002 I evaluated the past year and made my usual resolutions, some personal, some professional. I looked back fondly and ahead optimistically. The Governor's Residence was running at peak performance. Staff members had grown noticeably proficient in their duties. Events were organized, projects updated and much of the mansion had been renovated. We had just concluded another successful year of events, and a full calendar lie ahead for year 2002. I was excited for the year to come and resolved to finish the few remaining renovations, including improving outside lighting and safety at the Residence. I further resolved to run an even tighter ship because of the widening deficit I knew our state was facing.

My first year as Residence manager, I'd found ways to trim $10,000 from the mansion budget and created, with Terry's help, a rental policy that allowed nonprofits to use Residence space so long as they reimbursed the state for costs, saving the Residence even more money.

As I was preparing myself and staff for a leaner 2002 budget, I had no idea that the Governor was about to trim the fat by cutting myself, the Residence staff and the mansion itself out of the gubernatorial picture.

On January 3, 2002, the Governor gave his State of the State address from the Residence drawing room. A magnificent Italian marble fireplace served as a backdrop for what proved to be a dire, disconcerting speech about the state budget deficit totaling almost $2 billion.

The fallout regarding this news affected the Residence almost immediately. Being proactive, the Ventura administration announced it would cut the Governor's operating budget by 10 percent (a cut soon to be increased to 15-18 percent). The typical Residence budget was around $500,000 a year, and for the Residence, a 10 percent cut translated into a tighter belt in general plus the reduction of 1.5 positions.

Considering the workload and close-knit relationship the staff enjoyed, reducing positions was painfully difficult, but it had to be done. After many agonizing January discussions with Chief of Staff Steven Bosacker and the First Lady, we decided to eliminate one chef position and take one-quarter time from the second chef position and one-quarter time from a housekeeper's position (Beth Karlisch). Earlier, I had recommended that the First Lady's assistant (Mari Reed) be combined with an office personnel position, but Terry turned that idea down flat.

Since both chefs had worked through several administrations, the news that they would be leaving was especially discouraging. The cuts went into effect at the end of February, but because of a full calendar of events, the Residence workload remained heavy. We never canceled events; in fact, more were added to the schedule. Staff and caterers picked up the slack. In addition to their regular duties, housekeepers and office personnel often helped prepare meals for the First Family as well as for some events when the remaining chef was not on duty.

When the Governor discovered the culinary ramifications of his cuts, he came to me to express his concern, not for the chefs' well being but for his own. "Who's going to cook my meals?" he asked. I explained that the housekeepers and our steward Theresa would be cooking most meals. "But they're not chefs," he whined. I let the comment go and didn't bother to tell the Governor that Theresa and the housekeepers had been cooking some of his meals all along, especially the after-hour snacks he wolfed down.

The added duties often required staff to work overtime, despite the fact that there was no money in the budget to pay for extra hours. The additional time that hourly Residence workers put in was their donation to the state in 2002. Not one staff member complained to me about not being paid for extra hours—a true illustration of the loyalty and dedication the Residence staff had toward the Governor and the State of Minnesota.

In the midst of the cutbacks, Residence staff did get a pat on the back. Of course, it came not from the Governor but from the media. *Minnesota Monthly* magazine wrote a feature article that highlighted my position as Residence manager. It was a positive article with a full-page picture of me with the caption, "Man of the House: At the Governor's mansion, Dan Creed is indispensable, upstairs and downstairs." The role of the Governor's Residence manager is not commonly understood, since there are only 50 such positions nationwide, and I was pleased that, thanks to the article, Minnesotans would have a better understanding about what went on behind the closed gates of their Governor's Residence.

The article prompted several follow-up stories in other media, including the *St. Cloud Times*, which also interviewed Terry Ventura about my work. "Dan Creed is a very unique blend of class, warmth, poise, humor, intelligence and kindness," she said. Before Creed arrived for work in early 1999, Terry said she and others managed the phones, mail, filing system and everything else. "He came in and quickly pulled things together, earning the respect of (Terry) and the staff of 10."

With compliments like that, I never felt more secure in my job as I did that January. I had no inkling that instead of being "indispensable," as the *Minnesota Monthly* article put it, I and other Residence staff were all too dispensable to the Ventura administration. We never heard the ice cracking under our feet.

A LITTLE IN-SECURITY

The only person truly indispensable in Governor Ventura's eyes was the Governor himself.

Governor Ventura was always concerned, some say overly concerned, about the security of his family and his person. He always had a detail that followed his every move as well as security at both his Maple Grove and Governor's Residence homes. When he traveled, security went with him, even when his travels were not for state business. Though the Governor always insisted that sponsors such as the XFL reimbursed the state, the extra security travel left the impression that the Governor was overprotected at state expense.

I will say that this Governor—by nature of his celebrity status and abrasive nature, and as a result of his post-September 11th security concerns—probably did need more security than previous Governors. I do know that Governor Ventura regularly received death threats. Cassandra, who worked at the Capitol before the Residence, said the Governor received at least one threatening letter a week in her office alone, and that was at the beginning of the administration when Governor Ventura was well liked.

Head of Capitol Security for the Minnesota State Patrol, Tom Fraser, said protecting Jesse Ventura as governor was a greater challenge. Governor Ventura did receive more threats than other governors, Fraser told the *Minneapolis Star Tribune* April 21, 2003, There were 30 threats received in Governor Ventura's first 14 months in office, compared to the 19 threats that his predecessor, Governor Arne Carlson, received in three years. "There was nothing to compare to Ventura and security," Fraser told Mark Brunswick in the *Star Tribune* article. For example, "we were two-thirds of the way up a pyramid in Mexico and people were stopping him because they recognized who he was. I don't think (his successor) Pawlenty has that problem."

Regardless of the reasons, though, Governor Ventura's security costs were higher than previous administrations. At their highest, the state spent $1.43 million in 2001 on Governor Ventura security, more than twice what it spent to secure former Governor Arne Carlson, according to the *Star Tribune* article.

Whether or not the extra security Governor Ventura needed should have been paid for by the state was never an issue for me to argue. That was the Legislature's debate, and that was the problem. The Governor and Legislature worked together about as well as North and South Korea.

As the Legislature proposed ways to handle a budget deficit in the billions, the Governor vetoed their ideas. They shot back by overriding his vetoes—nine times that spring.

In February, legislators also raised their January request for 10 percent executive budget cuts up to 15-18 percent. Included in the additional percentage were cuts in the Governor's security budget.

Officially, the security cuts were part of budget deficit solu-

tion that lawmakers pushed through to override another gubernatorial veto. However, many suspected the cuts were made to
hit the Governor where it counted—his personal protection—as
a means of getting him to give in on other issues.

Specifically, legislators asked the Governor to cut his security force by some $175,000 in 2002. Those cutbacks would mean
the Governor could no longer afford, at state expense, to have
security at both his private home and at the Residence.
Governor Ventura was reportedly the first Minnesota governor
to ask the state to provide security at his private home.

Governor Ventura was furious that the Legislature would not
only leave him and his family in what he perceived to be great
danger but would overstep his authority to do it.

The Governor was especially angry with Senator Dean
Johnson, Chair of the House Transportation and Public Safety
budget committee who proposed the idea of cutting back on
gubernatorial security costs. Senator Johnson had long feuded
with the Governor and, more recently, had said he thought the
Governor was exaggerating his security needs.

Within minutes of attending a meeting where legislators told
him to trim security costs, the Governor was on the warpath to
Johnson's office to give the Senator a piece of the Ventura mind.

Johnson was on break in his office when "a breathless gubernatorial aid (Joe Ganoli) poked his head in the door. 'Dean get
out of here. The governor's coming your way, and he's upset,'"
St. Paul Pioneer Press newsman Jim Ragsdale reported in a Jan.
3, 2003, wrap-up article titled "Ventura's Legacy."

"Clad in a snowmobile jacket and brandishing an unlit cigar
stub (Ventura) arrived to confront his legislative tormentors,"
Ragsdale wrote. The Governor marched into Johnson's office
and blurted, "I'm here to tell you the Governor's mansion will
be closed the 30th of April. The reason is your $175,000 cut
from executive protection."

The Governor then crossed over to the Senator's office window
and pointed to a nearby stop sign and chastised Senator Johnson
for making fun of Governor Ventura's security concerns, Johnson
recalled in the Ragsdale story. "I see you said I thought Bin Laden
was hiding behind that stop sign here? Do you know, we have real
security issues in this state?" the Governor rumbled. Then, as if
trying to convey that senators should have security concerns of

their own, Governor Ventura (who has a concealed weapon carrying permit) pulled open his jacket and jeered at the Senator, "By the way, I'm not packing today."

A SHOCKING ANNOUNCEMENT

The still steaming Governor took his proclamation from Senator Johnson's office to the media and announced March 1, 2002, that he was closing the Governor's Residence and laying off the entire staff as of April 30, 2002. The announcement meant no staff or security would be at the official state Residence. The gates were to be locked and only minimal maintenance scheduled. The Governor stated that if there was no protection for the Residence, he would not stay there. He would instead use the state protection money at the Venturas' Maple Grove home.

The announcement came as a bombshell to nearly everyone, including Chief of Staff Bosacker and all Residence staff.

When the Governor made this announcement, some people in the Legislature and media thought he was calling legislators' bluff. Many were saying, "This could never happen; he will not close the Residence." Until the end, many staff thought it would not happen either because the decision seemed so wrong. The Residence, after all, was not just the Governor's home; it was the People's home.

The Governor failed to ever explain his decision to the staff affected by it. Like most Minnesotans, Residence staff knew little more about their position than what the Governor said to the press. We heard him say that he could cut our positions because we were "not part of the core administration," and we heard him say that if he needs to entertain at the Residence, "I can just order Dominoes® pizza." (We'd have been glad to save ourselves some meal preparation and dial the phone for him.)

Governor Ventura never once sat down with staff to tell us directly about the closing. As many times as we came in contact with the Governor around the Residence in the two months following his decision, Governor Ventura never brought up the subject to any of us. I even urged Steven to convince the Governor to speak to staff because I earnestly felt that his loyal but now injured and confused staff needed to hear directly from the Governor. Regrettably, that never happened.

When news of the Residence closing was announced,

Steven tried to reach me at home and on my cell phone and left several messages. Unfortunately, I was in a meeting and not available for several hours. When we did connect, Steven expressed his regrets and reiterated how professional and qualified the Residence staff was. He said he would certainly make those comments again later to the staff. Unfortunately, Steven failed to do so!

In fact, Steven was so focused on reaching me that he failed to notify all the staff about the closing announcement that day. While I found out via the answering machine, some Residence staff learned they were losing their jobs, and the mansion they loved, on the evening news.

Theresa and Cassandra, who were just leaving the Residence, did get a warning call from Steven less than three minutes before the TV news broke the story. He hadn't called to warn them specifically; he had called looking for me and mentioned it to them when they answered the phone instead. They urged Steven to call the other staff, but he explained that he had to get a hold of me, the staff's direct boss, first. No one else was notified, and the two staffers went to the security office to watch the TV report and learn the details there. After the broadcast, Cassandra called Sandy to talk over the news they'd just heard. But, Sandy hadn't heard the news yet. She and her husband had just returned home from taking their 17-year-old out for his birthday dinner when Cassandra called.

The news probably shocked Sylvia the most. She was in her kitchen at home when she heard her mother scream from the living room for her daughter to come look at the TV. Sylvia arrived in time to see a picture of the mansion with a chain imposed over the top. "They're shutting down the Residence," her dismayed mother reported.

I spoke with all staff that night by phone, and we were all in disbelief about how the closing was announced and especially about the idea that the closing could happen at all. We wondered how we had unknowingly wandered into No Man's Land between the gubernatorial and legislative forces.

After 10 days of agony and frustration regarding this news, Terry Ventura, Steven Bosacker, Director of Operations Paula Brown and I met with the staff at the Residence on March 11 to officially relay the closing news. The mood was somber as staff members received a letter from Steven stating that their appointment with the Governor's administration was ending. We were not fired, as the letter we received was the same letter that everyone in a Governor's office receives at the end of a term.

An emotional staff shed a lot of tears and shared their pain at the realization that all of our work—and the work of administrations before us—was going to be dismantled before our eyes. On top of that, the Residence staff had grown into a family, and we did not want to lose that special bond.

Once the tears subsided, we asked the obvious questions: Is there a chance this decision can be reversed? What can we do now to help it be reversed? Steven responded that our professional fates rested with the lawmakers. Legislators had cut the funding, and they would need to restore the money to keep the Residence open.

Terry, who cried throughout the meeting, vowed to call legislators, appear before committees, talk to the media and do whatever she could to get the funding restored. When asked if we should contact legislators, Steven told us it was fine for us to do so but added that he was not optimistic any effort on our part would pay off.

Staff also asked about the fate of Mari Reed, the First Lady's assistant, who was technically a member of the Residence staff. We learned that her position was exempt. Terry Ventura explained she felt justified in keeping a full-time assistant because her job as First Lady was not a paid position.

With the writing seemingly on the wall, housekeeper Beth Karlisch resigned to take another job because she needed a full-time position, and the remaining chef took a leave of absence and did not return. Sylvia Sanchez, administrative assistant, also soon found another job, but leaving the Residence was especially bittersweet for Sylvia because she loved her coworkers, the mansion and all of the American dreams it had represented to her and her immigrant mother.

By the end of March, only four staff were left to complete all the work during the Residence's remaining six weeks of operation. Somehow, we did it all! The housekeepers, Cassandra and Theresa did virtually all of the food preparation for the Venturas and prepared food for most of the smaller events as well. For larger events, we sought help from local chefs, such as those from the Hotel Sofitel, who donated their time since no monies were available to pay for their services. If possible, I tried to get a photo of the chefs with the Governor as a token of the state's appreciation; sadly, the Governor did not always accommodate even that simple request.

In the waning weeks, staff asked the Governor more than once if they should have any hope of the Residence remaining open. One morning, toward the end of March, he responded to Sandy's question with the same charge he'd given me, "Tell everyone to hang in there and not bail ship yet."

In reality, we should have tossed our bailing bucket overboard and jumped in after it, but staff took the Governor at his word and hung in there to the bitter end. We all kept the hope alive that funding would be restored and this nightmare would be over.

Hope was more than just a fantasy of desperate people clinging to a job and place they loved. Terry, legislators and, sometimes, even the Governor repeatedly told us there was hope. We believed them.

Following the March 11 staff meeting, I began to campaign legislators on staff's behalf via phone calls and e-mails. As Residence manager, I wanted to do everything I could for the staff and mansion I served.

I personally spoke with legislative leadership, including Speaker of the House Steve Sviggum, Senate Majority Leader Roger Moe and House Majority Leader—and future governor— Tim Pawlenty. Additionally, I contacted Senate budget committee members Doug Johnson and Richard Cohen. Everyone responded favorably and committed themselves to finding a resolution.

I was encouraged by my conversations—and by the fact the media and people of Minnesota seemed equally upset by the closing—that the Legislature might indeed find a fiscal solution for the Residence. After all, they had done so when the Governor had earlier threatened to close Fort Snelling. When people protested that closing, the Legislature found the money to keep it open. I now had reason to believe the Legislature would do the same for us.

I went to Steven Bosacker to share the good news. He was not elated. In fact, he was upset that I had contacted legislators without his knowledge. His contradiction shocked me, since he had personally given staff permission to contact legislators during the March 11 meeting. Instead of appreciating my proactive efforts, he demanded copies of the letters I had sent.

I was especially angered that Steven seemed to be turning his back on Residence staff because we staff had supported the Chief of Staff when he had been in trouble in November of 2000. At that time, Minnesota media broke a story that Steven had been charged with soliciting sexual favors from an undercover policeman in a downtown Minneapolis athletic facility steam room. Steven denied the charges, but the incident thrust the Ventura administration into negative publicity territory. The Chief of Staff took a few weeks off, and the Governor gave Steven his full support and welcomed him back. If the Governor gave Steven his support, I felt it proper for our staff to do the same. Knowing the importance of group support, I encouraged the Residence staff to send cards or e-mails to Steven to let him know we cared about him and were thinking of him as he struggled through the negative spotlight. Several Residence staff sent Steven cards of encouragement.

Based on Steven's reaction, I realized that the Residence staff would be on our own in trying to keep the mansion open. Capitol staff would not be doing much to help us.

A COLD VENTURA SHOULDER

As I continued to push lawmakers for help, I was getting anything but help from the Venturas.

On March 28, two couples from Wisconsin toured the Residence and commented to me about how terrible it was that the Governor was closing it. I simply agreed that it would be a shame to see the Residence closed.

The guests did not say anything different from what numerous other visitors had expressed on recent tours. The difference was that this time the Venturas' son, Tyrel, was upstairs and overheard the conversation. He considered the comments degrading to his dad and phoned his mother twice to relay the visitors' discussion. Terry was upset and wanted to know, "Is Dan saying anything negative?" According to Terry, Tyrel said, "No."

Early the next morning, Terry called me at the office. She was obviously angry about the comments and asked me why I did not throw the guests out of the house. I explained I could not throw someone out of a public house simply for something they said. People have the freedom to voice their opinions even if they disagree with the Governor.

I further discussed a growing concern I had about the closing, based on a comment the Governor had made to security. He told them he was going to "lock the Residence and strip the contents down to the light bulbs." I was pained to hear that the staff's efforts to organize and maintain the decorum of the Residence would have been in vain and that all the fine furniture we'd so carefully restored and cared for would be put in storage or returned to donors. I was more pained to learn later that, as a result of my conversation with the First Lady regarding the Governor's comments, superiors reprimanded several security officers for talking. From that time forward, the security team was close-lipped regarding any information, and this made my job more challenging because I relied on information from security about changes in the Governor's schedule that affected the Residence.

During this same conversation with Terry, I learned she was also upset about arrangements for an upcoming lunch she was hosting because her assistant Mari Reed had said that staff was being uncooperative about setting a date for the lunch. I informed the First Lady—and learned that Mari had failed to tell her—that they wanted the lunch on the same day as the Residence was hosting a dinner for the Canadian ambassador, and a double event schedule would be taxing an already stretched staff.

The First Lady and I reached no real understanding, and I remained frustrated after our conversation. I called Steven Bosacker and asked to see him as soon as possible. He said to come over immediately. By the time I arrived at his Capitol office, Terry had called Steven and complained to him about the Residence staff, relaying to him the same issues she had discussed with me.

During a 90-minute meeting with Steven and Director of Operations Paula Brown, I reiterated my frustrations over how Tyrel, Mari Reed and the First Lady seemed to be misinterpreting the actions of a loyal, hardworking staff. I was frustrated as well, I told Steven, that the First Lady did not seem to be cutting staff any slack despite our reduced numbers and added pressures over losing our jobs. I hoped she would be more supportive. Steven's only response was that perhaps the Residence should have closed sooner than April 30!

During this same meeting, Steven and I discussed the Residence closure proceedings. For the remaining weeks in April, we had a full schedule of events on the calendar, and the staff was eager to accommodate every scheduled group. However, we knew we had much to do to prepare the mansion for what could be a long closure since we did not know when, or if, the Residence would reopen for public use.

At the end of the meeting, Steven shocked me again when he told me that I "was on a different track" regarding the Residence closure than the administration. Not understanding what he meant, I reiterated my conviction that the Residence did not have to close, and it was not in the best interest of the state. I relayed my optimism that legislators would do something before the 11th hour to provide funding, and I felt that the letters and phone calls I made to them kept our chances alive. Steven did not agree but had to go to another meeting and didn't have time to explain his "different track" comment further.

By this point in the pre-closure timetable, Terry Ventura had grown weary of defending the decision to close the Residence. In one interview, obviously irritated at being asked repeatedly about the fate of staff, the First Lady coldly stated, "Thousands of others are losing their jobs in the state." Residence staff knew that, of course, but we were still hurt when we read her words because we thought we were not just in the category of "all the others." The staff had, we believed, always enjoyed a special, close relationship with Terry Ventura. Regretfully, it appeared our unique bond had been broken.

Ironically, that same afternoon, Senate Majority Leader Roger Moe called me to lend encouragement, saying he knew that it was a tough time for the Residence but to hang in there. He reiterated that he felt funding would be restored and was complimentary to staff, saying, "Your staff does a great job! …This should not be happening to you guys."

A few nights later, House Majority Leader Tim Pawlenty called me at my home. He was kind and supportive with his comments. Pawlenty had been at the Residence on several occasions and certainly was aware of the staff's quality work.

Then, in late April, well-known Minnesota politician Norm
Coleman, who ran against Jesse Ventura for governor in 1998,
visited the Residence as the featured speaker at a Minnesota
Builders Association breakfast meeting. Coleman took time to
thank me for my hospitality and congratulate staff on the "great
job you did in the face of unbelievable circumstances." He com-
miserated with everyone that morning, repeatedly saying that,
"Closing the Residence is a big mistake!"

With all these powerful legislators seemingly coming out on
our side, I was beginning to feel more optimistic about the
Residence's and staff's future. While the Governor still had the
right to close the mansion, the Legislature might restore the
funding that would change his mind or reword the legislation to
take the power away from him and reopen the mansion.

On April 25, Senators Cohen and Johnson sent a letter to the
Governor imploring him to keep the Residence open until May
20th. "We personally do not believe closing the mansion is
philosophically or financially the right thing to do," they wrote.
"As you very well know, the Residence is the 'house of the people' and remains important to our state's ongoing history. We
believe it is in the best interest of the state to keep the
Residence open for official state business and ceremonies. The
Residence staff has dedicated their time and energy to maintain
the Residence, and we believe it is important that they remain
employees of the state. At a minimum, we would ask that you
delay your decision to close the Residence until the final 2002-
03 budget negotiations have concluded. If you do, we will see
that the Residence is given serious consideration for additional
funds to remain open to the public."

As I shared this news and words of encouragement with staff,
we all felt bolstered that all would not be lost in the end. The
Governor would surely hear the outcry and change his mind
despite the fact that he would then have to admit to actually
making a mistake. And, if Governor Ventura wasn't man enough
to do that, then at least our legislators would not let a bully shut
down the people's house. After all, legislators had promised the
Governor, the public and us just that.

Toward the end of April, staff got the most encouraging news
yet. Earlier in the month, legislators had requested a ruling from
the attorney general as to whether or not the Governor could

actually close the Residence. Just before the April 30 shut-down day, the attorney general ruled, "The fact that the Governor asserts that his budget is insufficient to operate the Residence is not a basis to 'close' it." In fact, Minnesota Statute 16B.271 Subd. 1 requires that the Governor's Residence must be made available for official ceremonial functions of the state. Accordingly, the attorney general ruled, "the commissioner of administration must continue to **maintain** the Residence in a manner that permits its availability and use for ceremonial functions."

For a moment, the Governor appeared to acquiesce from his "shut it down" stand, when John Wodele issued a press release that, to comply with the ruling, the Governor's Residence would remain "available" for official ceremonial functions and be "maintained" according to acceptable state standards.

I was crushed, however, moments later when I learned that the partially opened Residence would not be staffed.

In spite of the letter from Senators Cohen and Johnson, in spite of the public outcry and in spite of the attorney general's ruling, there was no spirit of compromise from the Governor. He was not willing to meet anyone halfway, even after legislators promised Residence funding.

The Residence would close April 30, end of discussion.

THE APRIL COUNTDOWN

Staff were not the only people saddened by the Residence dilemma. Members of the 1006 Society, which had been responsible for returning the mansion to its original splendor, were heartbroken to learn their years of hard work would be for naught if the Residence was closed.

The members of this group held their last official board meeting before the Residence closed in April. As a an advisor to that board, I attended the meeting and heard firsthand how angry, distraught and concerned Society members were about the future of the property they loved. Many had worked for decades to raise funds to improve the Residence, and they believed the Governor was dismantling that work.

Terry did not attend this meeting, but did call to stress again that "closing the Residence was not the Governor's fault. It was the legislators'." Not all of the 247 society members were convinced, and there were grumblings among membership that the Governor was indeed to blame. When the "negative" comments reached the First Lady's ears, she asked me to send a letter on her behalf to all 1006 Society members reiterating her earlier comments.

The reality of a closing was, by now, sinking in within the society and the Residence. So too was the reality that no one in the Ventura administration or family cared a great deal about how much the closing would affect staff and others.

Staff received that message loud and clear the afternoon of April 4 during what would be our last monthly meeting with Capitol staff. Unbelievably, not one comment was made during this meeting about the Residence staff's departure. Cassandra, Sylvia and I attended and were all shocked to hear no words of appreciation or good-bye, nothing from Steven Bosacker or anyone else to indicate this was the Residence staff's last meeting. Traditionally, when employees left the Governor's staff, some kind of recognition was planned. This time nothing had been done to acknowledge the departure of seven Residence employees. I later heard from Capitol staff that several of them had suggested throwing a farewell party but that Steven had inexplicably turned down the idea. He chose to say nothing at all.

April 9 proved a telling day for the few remaining Residence staff as well. The Canadian Ambassador was invited to an elegant Beef-Wellington dinner in the evening, and the First Lady's charity had finally been scheduled for that afternoon. All of the guests, including Canadian General Counsel Susan Thompson and former Vice President Walter Mondale and his wife, seemed pleased with the events and the Residence. Staff was especially pleased with the success of the dinner. Guests had stayed late into the evening and, knowing this was our last official function at the Residence, staff was happy to see everyone enjoying themselves.

The only person who appeared unhappy that day was Terry. She never spoke to any staff during the luncheon event and did not attend the ambassador dinner. Most telling, the First Lady did not even say good-bye when she left, an unprecedented exit. We could only conclude that whatever was truly bothering the First Lady was beyond our repair, at least for the time being. Staff guessed that she could still be upset about incidents between the staff and Mari Reed, including Sylvia's refusal to hug the assistant and my concerns about hosting the charity lunch on the same day as the ambassador dinner. We also believed that Terry was feeling the pressure of the media attention and blame that the Governor's decision to close the Residence had brought her.

I decided to give the First Lady space and time to resolve her emotions and did not call her for several days.

CLOSING THE GATES

The final weeks in April were jam packed, not only with daily events, but also with completing the many details of closing the Residence. Staff prioritized every minute of every day.

The staff had to pack and store a mansion full of items, dispose of perishable goods, inventory all fixed assets, and even move live plants into the solarium so someone assigned from Capitol staff could water them.

One of my tasks was to move all liquor from inside the Residence to the basement under the garage. Since it was not clear who would have access to the mansion after staff left, I wanted to secure the stock of liquor. It was a move that both Steven Bosacker and Paula Brown approved.

In the last days, every Minnesota media outlet featured the closing of the Residence as their lead story. Numerous stations called Communications Director John Wodele to gather information on the closing proceedings. John, as he traditionally did, sent them to me because I was the best source to articulate day-to-day mansion details. I did dozens of radio, television and newspaper interviews, and every reporter wanted to know how staff felt and if any of us disagreed with the closing. At that time, we all answered with basically the same short response: We were sad to see the Residence close and wished there could be another way of resolving the issue regarding funding.

Each staff member tried extremely hard to not say anything contrary to the Governor's views. During one interview I was doing with WCCO's Pat Kessler, Tyrel called his mom to let her know I was talking to Pat. Terry called Cassandra at the Residence and told her to get a message to me right away. Cassandra interrupted the interview to give me a note from Terry, which read, "Be careful with what you say to Pat Kessler.

He is a snake in the grass." I never relayed that message to Pat
Kessler, who I always felt was honest and professional in his
conversations and interviews, and continued with the interview.

Between April 26 and April 29 several media requested permission to film the removal of loaned art pieces, including
paintings and furniture, from the Residence. John Wodele gave
his permission.

Of all the pieces we packed up and moved out, I most regret-
ted watching a 16th Century, eight-sided European table leave
the Residence because I was afraid the museum that loaned the
piece might not do so when the Residence reopened. The table
had been such an elegant centerpiece in the foyer for more than
10 years. Months later, I read in the newspaper that my fears
were realized. The table did not return.

As staff carried some items outside to waiting vans, I felt as
if we were all part of a bizarre funeral procession. Cameramen
filmed each step of the somber scene, and as I carried each
piece, the finality of the situation finally sunk in. Many people
had warned me that this would be how it would end, but I had
wanted to believe that the family we had served so well would
not let us down and that the legislators who served the people
and the people's house would not fail the people. The reality
that neither had come through for staff was painful indeed.

The media, who filmed all day Friday, returned Monday
morning to record the final packing. They would not be allowed
to stay long. The Governor returned to the Residence at noon
to watch *The Young and the Restless*, nearly oblivious to the
soap opera unfolding all around him. He was irritated to see the
media inside his "private walls" and was clearly annoyed when
a few reporters tried to ask him questions. After he went
upstairs, the Governor called John Wodele to complain about
the reporters and told him he wanted everyone "to get out and
stay out." John called and relayed the order to me and added,
"immediately." I ushered the press outside and, from then on,
all reporting of the Residence closure had to be done from outside the gates.

The last day proved to be more emotional than I imagined
possible. I was up early to accommodate TV station requests to
interview me in front of the mansion during their 6 a.m. news
programs. As I drove in, I felt an avalanche of emotions: hurt,

anger, misuse and especially betrayal. By this time, Terry had not spoken directly to me for several weeks, and I wondered often if she understood how we all felt. That day I worried most of all that she would not even come to say good-bye.

A convoy of reporter vans greeted me as I arrived. I noticed that former Governor Arne Carlson and his wife were also out front doing an interview. I completed my two interviews and then walked over and thanked the former Governor for the support for keeping the Residence open that he had expressed in his interview.

Within minutes, an obviously irritated John Wodele called me on my cell phone. He wanted to know why the Carlsons were out front. I explained that they were doing an interview, but I had not invited them. He implied that I had, but I was as surprised as anyone when I pulled up that morning and saw them there. Besides, I thought, isn't the Residence and the sidewalk in front of it a public place and, as Minnesota citizens, aren't Governor Carlson and his wife allowed to stand there?

John then related that he was equally upset to learn from security that Mrs. Olivia Dodge, who had donated her family home to the state decades ago, was coming to the Residence in the afternoon. He did not want her there, especially because of the media attention her visit would draw—as if the vans full of reporters didn't qualify as "media attention" already!

The Governor's communications director was still upset about comments Mrs. Dodge had made at a news conference the day before when she expressed her outrage at the Residence closing. "Now, at the 11th hour, I am glad to say how I feel. I feel very sad. Maybe I shouldn't use the word, but betrayed. It's been handled very badly," reported Peg Meier in the *Minneapolis Star Tribune*. "This gift that we thought would be of great benefit to the state is being tossed back and forth between the Legislature and the Governor like a football."

I confirmed to John that Mrs. Dodge had requested to see the house one final time before it was locked up. "Yes," I said, "she is coming by for a tour with her son and daughter-in-law." John insisted, "That's not a good idea" and implied that I should cancel her visit. I replied that I felt that the family who donated the house had every right to see it again whenever they wanted.

John went to far as to imply that Mrs. Dodge's visit was another media ploy by staff to get attention. This could not have been further from the truth. I did not even know that Mrs. Dodge wanted to come to the Residence until the day before when she herself called me and asked if she could make one last tour.

Though he was the director of communications, John never came to the Residence during the final days and instead sent a staff member to monitor what was being said. That staffer also presented Mrs. Dodge with a press release later that day that detailed the Governor's official reasons for closing the Residence. This attempt to appease Mrs. Dodge seemed weak and unprofessional, and I was embarrassed for the administration in their dealings with such a fine and noble benefactor.

When Mrs. Dodge arrived that morning, she spoke to reporters at the gate, reiterating her disappointment with the Residence's closing. She then came inside, greeted staff, and posed for several photos with us. At this moment, the First Lady unexpectedly arrived to pack some of her personal belongings. She joined the staff on the tour, took a photo with Mrs. Dodge and then went upstairs to pack.

We opened a bottle of champagne to celebrate the staff's accomplishments and to toast Mrs. Dodge for her support. Staff was especially touched when the Irvine family matriarch complimented our efforts to maintain her birth home. "When the Residence reopens, I want a blown-up photo of you hung on the wall to honor what you have done for this place," she told us that morning.

Among those receiving compliments were staff members who had departed in March for other jobs, after the closing had been announced. I had invited them back that afternoon so we could all say good-bye to each other and so that all staff could have some closure to this painful experience.

John Wodele was especially irritated that staff members who had already departed had been invited back and again accused us of trying to arrange media sympathy. I told him just as strongly that it was right for staff to be here. They had poured their sweat and souls, as I had, into serving the Venturas and the Residence, and they needed the closure the day would bring. I reiterated that I had no intention of making a media spectacle of the situation. An important piece of our lives was taken from us, and we wanted to say good-bye together. That was all.

The Governor's communications director saved the best part of my dressing down for last. He let me know in no uncertain terms that my comment in the newspaper that morning was "out of line." I had not seen the paper and had no idea to what comment he was referring. He read the quote to me as, "The Governor should not be making the decision to close the Residence." I was confused since I did not remember saying it that way and thought I'd said, "It's a shame the Governor's decision led to the closing of the Residence." As someone who had heard Governor Ventura's rantings for four years about how the newspapers never quoted him correctly, John insisted that this time the paper must have gotten it right. This is what I must have said. "Not every quote is correct in the newspaper," I stressed, but he would not let up.

I explained that my concern was having this Governor, or any governor, in a position where they would need to close the Residence because of budget concerns. My statements in the interview tied into my long-held belief that the Governor's Residence should not be under the control of the Governor's office.

Apparently not comprehending what I said, John acknowledged that I had freedom of speech, but that if an employee of the Governor publicly disagrees with the Governor's policies, that employee is being disloyal and should resign. (I thought, resign what? Hadn't I already lost my job!)

I didn't disagree with John, though, and tried again to convey that I was not disagreeing with the Governor either. In fact, I was trying to be supportive by saying that the Governor should not have been faced with such a decision in the first place.

We hung up without a resolution. I was still fuming and still trying to juggle all the work of the last-day media, packing and staff needs, when Steve Bosacker called me around 10 a.m. He was equally upset based on what John Wodele had just conveyed to him of our conversation.

I was frustrated and perplexed and told Steven that I did not appreciate John saying any staff member, or I, was disloyal to the Governor. "Well, we only know what we read in the paper, Dan," Steven replied. I was amazed to hear such a statement from someone I knew had been misquoted in various publications in the past.

I again explained why I felt it was right to include the former

JESSE: THE BETRAYOR | 155

staff and honor Mrs. Dodge's request to return to the Residence. When I finished, Steven simply said, "Carry on." He added that he might come to say good-bye to staff, and I encouraged him to do so. Regretfully, he never did and staff were insulted by his absence. He was, after all, our boss.

As that last day wound to a close, staff began to gather for a final farewell. We had asked Terry to join us, but I wasn't sure she would, given the emotional state of our relationship the previous few weeks. I was truly elated when the First Lady and Tyrel dropped in to say goodbye. Jade later called in a heartfelt farewell.

We all held hands in a circle and each person said his or her good-byes. Terry wished everyone well, gave each person a hug amidst all the tears and then said how she wanted to invite everyone for a barn party in Maple Grove that summer.

The Governor came home about that time, and Terry asked him to join us. He shook hands with everyone and said "thanks." This was an unexpected gesture and a welcomed one. It gave staff a glimmer of hope that we could leave on good terms and perhaps return to work once the Governor straightened out the funding issues with the Legislature. Being the eternal optimist, I hoped for a quick resolution to the whole political turmoil so we staff could return to what we loved, taking care of the First Family and the "Big House."

At 5 p.m. on April 30, 2002, the Residence staff's appointments with the Governor's office officially ended. I made a final walk-through of the Residence with much sadness as I pondered how all the fun and hard work we'd poured into three and a half years was a thing of the past. Where beautiful paintings once hung, walls were barren; where dignitaries once sat, dust would now gather.

At the end of the day, Department of Administration Commissioner David Fisher, whose department oversees the Residence property, joined Governor's Residence Council President Sam Grabarski for a final inspection of the Residence and to address to the media. Fisher explained the administration's reasoning for closing the Residence, restating the cause was lack of funding for security. In other words, I thought, the Governor decided to pull the security blanket off his staff in order to sew a stronger blanket for himself.

When Fisher finished speaking with the media, reporters asked for me. I was feeling renewed hope after our farewell with the Governor and First Lady and was eager to leave everything on a positive note. When one reporter asked me how staffs' relationship was with the Venturas, I responded by saying, "It could not be better," a sentiment I sincerely meant in that moment.

The actual last interaction between staff members and the media that day probably proved to be the final undoing for any hope that staff would return to their jobs. Unbeknownst to me until that very moment, Theresa, Cassandra, Sylvia and Sandy decided that they too wanted to talk to reporters—not to complain about their predicament but to simply thank the media for its support of the staff and of keeping the Residence open.

The quartet locked arms and walked down the driveway to the gate where media waited. Indeed, most Minnesota media had been supportive and sympathetic to all the staff. The photo of the women arm-in-arm made virtually every television news program and newspaper front page statewide. The public reaction was overwhelming in sympathy for the staff and in disdain for the Governor's actions.

The Governor's office immediately accused the now former staff of conspiring to create a media stunt that made the Governor look bad. Much was made of the fact that the ladies had worn red, white and blue outfits and had locked arms "in solidarity." The women have since assured me that their decision was a spur-of-the-moment choice born of the emotions of the day. They had given no organized thought to what they wore that morning and only locked arms as a way of supporting each other as they walked and cried their way out of the gates of the mansion they'd considered a home.

A DISTURBING ENCORE

The April 30 closing was traumatic, but the emotional roller coaster staff had just ridden would seem tame compared to the heartache and betrayals we were about to ride in the aftermath.

I felt all along that public sentiment would not allow for a long closure of the Residence and strongly urged the Ventura administration to consider several options to prevent the dismantling of the Residence because I believed that reopening a completely closed Residence could be quite costly.

One option I suggested to Steven and Paula was to leave one housekeeper on staff to keep the house clean and secure, thereby avoiding having to remove the loaned art pieces and furniture and enabling a turn-key reopening. I also suggested that the Governor could place all the staff on a leave of absence, without pay, until the reopening. This would not cost the state any money, and if a reopening occurred quickly, experienced staff would be in place for a smooth transition.

Neither of my suggestions were accepted. Instead, the administration spent thousands to dismantle the Residence, pay out staff vacation time, disconnect phone lines, cancel orders and have vendors pick up leased equipment the latter two of which often created contract penalties to pay. When the Residence eventually reopened, I knew all these costs would come again, in reverse, as everything was reinstalled and rerented. If new staff had to be hired or trained, costs would go higher. Even little details could be expensive. For example, had gardener Bill Suchy been able to order plants when he wanted to in early spring, the state would have gotten them at wholesale. By waiting until summer—when the mansion might be reopened—the state would have to pay retail, a difference of some $1,100.

Though my suggestions fell on deaf ears, former Residence staff continued to expect that we would soon be back to work. Even if Governor Ventura did not reopen the mansion, surely his soon-to-be elected successor would.

I continued to work earnestly to assist in reopening the Residence and push for the rehiring of staff. I solicited help from the two gubernatorial candidates, Democrat Roger Moe and Republican Tim Pawlenty. When I spoke with each of them in person, they both voiced support and later stated publicly they wanted to rehire the staff if elected. I contacted business leaders for their advice and support as well.

The week following the closure, Paula Brown, Ventura's director of operations, called and asked for a copy of my master's thesis on *How To Run a Governor's Residence*. I made a copy for her because it was always my intent to leave a "how to" manual for the next manager so he or she would have a guideline to follow.

That same week, I had an encouraging conversation with Administration Commissioner David Fisher. He asked me if I was still interested in the Residence manager's job, to which I replied an emphatic, "Yes!" Fisher was trying to be proactive, based on a proposal the Legislature was contemplating regarding future administration of the Residence. The proposal was to allocate funding for the Residence, but place the responsibility of the facility under the Department of Administration instead of the Governor's office.

All other state properties are under the Department of Administration, and it seemed logical that the Residence also be. The proposal could prevent a future governor from being faced with the trauma of closing the Residence due to budget cuts. More importantly, it could mean the Residence would never again be a political pawn. This is similar to how the White House is administered through a separate operational expenditures budget managed by Congress' Office of Management and Budget. Under that system, White House employees are considered civil servants, and their jobs are protected with each new administration. The President may choose to replace someone, such as the Clintons did with the executive chef, but an employee would be transferred to another department instead of let go.

David asked me to do some research regarding this concept, so I talked with my White House counterpart Gary Walters, who worked at the U.S. Residence for 30 years and for several presidents. The system provides continuity in operating the Residence and saves the government from having to train a new staff every four years. Walters also explained that the staff is professional and can serve a first family, regardless of staff's political persuasion. A case in point is a close friend of mine who worked as a head White House housekeeper for more than 25 years. Her home in the foothills of the Smoky Mountains showcases hundreds of photos of her with presidents from Roosevelt through Nixon. As she often says, "I was loyal to each of the families, even though I did not always agree with their lifestyles." I had felt the same about my First Family.

Also at David's request, I drew up a budget with the minimum requirements needed to reopen the Residence; a legislative analyst evaluated the budget figures I proposed. Throughout this process, I was optimistic that our efforts would result in rehiring the staff. That certainly was David's intention, though nothing had been officially stated. David emphasized he wanted to be prepared to move quickly if the Legislature provided the funding and placed the Residence under his responsibility.

The Legislature provided that funding May 18, 2002, when it passed the budget bill. At first, I was elated until David and I realized that the measure to pass control of the Residence to the Department of Administration had been deleted. Residence control remained under the Governor's hands. I later learned that Steven Bosacker pushed particularly hard to ensure this, and the legislators consented.

Then, shortly after the budget passed, John Wodele announced that the Governor would reopen the Residence. My heart skipped a beat and then sunk with his next statement. The mansion would reopen but probably not until August to give the administration time to rewrite staff job descriptions. He ominously added, it was not certain if staff would be rehired.

In response, several former staff members e-mailed Steven to inquire about the status of Residence staff. He never responded to their inquiries. Though most staff had already procured new or temporary jobs, we all wanted to return because of the great passion we had for the Residence and its care.

Steven didn't need to respond anyway. It was ludicrous to imagine that job descriptions needed to be rewritten for former staff. The administration had obviously already determined the staff would not be rehired. That is why Steven lobbied hard to retain control over the Residence, so he could hire a new staff. This was extremely discouraging; however, it was what we had come to expect.

On Friday evening, June 1, Steven Bosacker finally telephoned me to give me the news officially. Steven said that he was responding to my messages and that I would not like the news. He simply told me, "It has been decided to have a fresh start at the Residence."

When I pressed him to explain "a fresh start," I received only silence.

When I asked the obvious question, "Did we do something wrong? Was it about the media the last day? Was it about the earlier Tyrel confrontation?" Steven only reiterated that, "The decision has been to start fresh."

Needless to say, this conversation was extremely frustrating. I pleaded that staff deserved an explanation especially considering the kind of work a depleted staff did for the Governor the last two months. Again, the response was silence.

I phoned the other staff to break the news to them myself, though Steven also phoned a few of the staff. When he spoke to Theresa and used the term "clean slate was needed," Theresa asked, " Is the old one dirty?" He said, "Oh, no, this has nothing to do with job performance." That conversation with Steven would be the only explanation Residence staff ever received.

Theresa probably felt the strongest betrayal because she had the closest staff relationship with the Venturas and got along with Mari Reed. She had never said a bad word about the family, or anybody else, especially to the media. She felt especially betrayed because the Governor himself had reassured her that she would be all right in all of this. When she asked him why the closure, he said, "T", it's all the damn Legislature's fault. If it was up to me..." She was so sure she would be called back that she only took on-call temporary jobs and didn't even pursue full-time work.

Other staff's reaction was the same as mine. I felt hurt, angry and especially betrayed. I knew the Governor was ultimately responsible but also knew that Steven and Terry shared much of the blame. Steven and Terry both had great influence with the Governor, and if either of them had truly wanted us back, we would have been back.

Terry certainly could have talked the Governor into keeping the staff if she wanted. In fact, the Governor had all but told us that it was, ultimately, his wife's decision. During the post-closing weeks, I had called Terry and asked her to call me back. She never did. I also formally requested a meeting with the Governor. His reply was a simple "no" that this is a "matter for the First Lady to decide."

I can only guess as to why the First Lady betrayed us with her silence. Perhaps she was still upset about the incidents with Mari, perhaps her opinion of staff had been poisoned by her assistant's reports, perhaps she was still miffed because staff took issue with Tyrel's behavior or perhaps she felt staff had betrayed her husband by talking to the media on the day of the closing.

Because I admired her and considered her a friend, the First Lady's betrayal stings the most to this day. There was nothing we wouldn't have done for the First Lady, and she repaid our loyal service by hiding the truth. She sat across from us crying elephant-sized tears and sharing our pain at the Residence closing. She cried with us as she lied to us.

The truth was finally obvious to all of us. Closing the Residence and getting rid of staff had been not only the Governor's idea but the First Lady's preference all along.

Their thoughtless act cost taxpayers thousands of dollars and cost citizens the opportunity to enjoy the Residence because numerous scheduled events were canceled, no new bookings made for the summer and thousands of visitors turned away from tours. And, it cost 10 Residence staff their jobs and dignity. Ironically, though, it was probably the Governor who suffered the greatest fallout. The closing of the Residence and related stories became the biggest political liability of his career, and some political pundits speculate that this issue alone led to Governor Ventura's June conclusion and announcement that he would not to seek reelection.

It now became clear what Steven Bosacker meant back in April when he told me I was on a "different track" than the administration regarding the closing of the Residence. The legislators had placed the Governor in an awkward position, and they would have to pay. It appeared it was to be tit for tat. Closing the Residence was apparently the best way to make the Legislature look bad. The entire situation involving the Residence closure had been a political game, and Residence staff were the pawns.

NO HAPPY ENDING

The Monday following Wodele's announcement, the media picked up the story and immediately started interviewing staff members. I received calls from all over the state. My cell phone never stopped ringing, and several television crews interviewed me at Normandale Community College, where I was teaching summer classes. The media all asked the same questions, "Why?" Because no one had ever—nor still has ever—answered that question for me, I had no answer to give them.

Without putting words in his mouth, I could only speculate that the issues John Wodele voiced on the last day, April 30, had something to do with the decision. John, of course, denied this reasoning but never elaborated on any other reasons, except to say that I had "said things that were not supportive of the Governor's budgetary decisions." (Apparently, I was only supposed to tell people how happy and excited I was that I and my staff were losing our jobs.)

During several days in early June, former staff answered questions but never once betrayed any loyalties or the Venturas' privacy. We had always been protective of them, even after they threw us overboard.

Then, in the midst of the closing uproar, the media were tipped off about a Web site that featured pictures of Tyrel's parties that one guest/friend had taken over the years and posted on the site. I didn't learn about the Web site until I started hearing media stories about alleged parties. Then, one day when the parties were the subject of speculation on a talk radio show, a former Residence employee—who had left the Residence a year before the closing—phoned in and confirmed the rumors. She related how housekeepers had to clean up after Tyrel's parties and late-night guests and talked about damaged furniture, suspicious activities and the Stewart Peters debacle.

The cat was out of the bag and running at top speed across the state.

Again, the media contacted former Residence staff members to ask for verification. For several days, staff refused to comment. Then, as we should have predicted, the Ventura administration blamed Residence staff for leaking the stories as a way to get even for not being hired back.

Some media also accused staff of being liars because we had changed our stories about the Venturas since the day of the closing. That day we'd said our relationship with the Venturas was fine. That was true, then. Several weeks later, circumstances and staff opinions of the Venturas had changed, since we realized how they had betrayed Residence staff.

Several of us consulted an attorney. Because all kinds of rumors were exploding about the goings-on inside the Residence, our attorney recommended staff clarify for the media what we knew to be true and what was not true.

In spite of our efforts, the staff was still blamed for leaking the stories in large part because media sound bites left the impression that Residence staff were breaking the story instead of responding to it.

Wodele said in the *Minneapolis Star Tribune*, "this was the effort of a disgruntled staff trying to get back at the Governor," and that "I was fired for incompetence."

There are several amazing things about these statements. First of all, John knew I was not fired. He also knew firsthand that I was professional and that my work ethic was excellent. He also was aware that the Governor, First Lady and Chief of Staff had all given staff members glowing letters of recommendation just two weeks before the closing. Furthermore, while it's safe to say that Residence staff were disappointed, hurt and frustrated over the turn of events, none of the staff employed in 2002 went to the media, nor did we ask anyone else to do so in our stead. Although this staff was aware of the incidents regarding Tyrel, we remained loyal to the Governor and his family.

Then, the administration's response got more personal than I could have imagined. Wodele told Minnesotans in a KARE TV 10 p.m. report by Kerri Miller, anchored by newswoman Diana Pierce, that I was a "sick person."

Both John Wodele and I, as well as Sylvia Sanchez, had been interviewed for the story. I was asked to confirm or deny reports of broken furniture, cigarette burns, vomit stains and unapproved office computer use during Tyrel's parties. I responded that "Obviously, there is evidence of some kind of partying going on."

John, when told that I confirmed the parties, questioned my credibility as a man "who's obviously hurt and in a vindictive mood since he is not being rehired at the Residence."

When the interview delved into the closing itself, I responded to the reporter's request for my opinion on the closing and decision not to rehire staff.

"A grave wrong has been committed here," I told her. "They know it. They absolutely know it and they need to do the right thing, and that's apologize to each and every one of us."

Sylvia echoed my sentiments and defended my position in all that had unfolded. "To stand and listen to him (Dan) be called, plain and simple, a liar is just demeaning and totally, totally wrong."

When told of our comments, Wodele had one of his own. After expressing that the Venturas were outraged that staff was making the allegations about Tyrel, he added, Dan Creed is "a sick man who ought to be going to church to get counseling instead of holding press conferences."

Though that particular comment burned worse than others, I was bolstered by the overwhelming support I received from Minnesotans across the state. Cards and e-mails arrived by the dozens and people even called me at home. One phone message from an unknown caller simply said, "You have done the State of Minnesota a great service. Thank you!"

National media covered the story, including articles in the *Wall Street Journal* and *People* magazine, and the majority of media were extremely supportive and sympathetic to former staff. In addition, I was encouraged by the legislators I ran into in the months after the closing to continue to keep my chin up. They often thanked me for being courageous and protective of the state's property.

Throughout the months after the closing, the former staff also stayed in touch, lending support and encouragement as we all tried to move on with our lives.

Then, the Venturas reopened the Governor's Residence and all the old wounds.

In mid-August, the First Family announced that a new Residence manager had been hired. This news disappointed me because I had applied for my old position. Of course, I would not get an interview, even though I had letters of recommendation from the Governor, Terry, Steven Bosacker and even the 1006 Society.

Because they hadn't run a Residence before, the new staff had lots of questions. For example, one day Paula Brown called a former employee to ask how to turn the dishwasher on. Another time, security called one of my staff to inquire about turning on the outside speakers. Calls like this would not have been necessary had the administration at least rehired one or two of the former staff.

With five months left of the term, the decision to hire all new staff not only cost the state thousands of dollars but, from a business and operational standpoint, was illogical.

When Governor Ventura announced that summer that he would not seek reelection after returning from June trip to

China, the Governor tried to explain that he did not rehire the former staff because he had already decided not to run for reelection before his trip. He suggested, "Won't they (the staff) feel foolish?" There was no logic to his reasoning. Why should the Governor hire a new staff for five months if he is not seeking reelection and knows that his successor may well not keep the same staff.

The answer is: closing the Residence and terminating its staff was never a logical decision. It was a knee-jerk reaction by a vindictive man with the power to see it through. It is indeed sobering to realize the extent that one Governor can go to exact revenge upon his enemies real, and imagined, and to realize how little the state's most powerful man cared about the taxpayers, the state's image and the people who had dedicated their time, talents and themselves to serve him so well.

SAME OLD STORY

Believe it or not, Residence staff continued to have some hope of getting their jobs back even after all the dirty water had run over the Ventura dam.

Legislators, and specifically the two top contenders to replace Governor Ventura as Minnesota Governor that November—Tim Pawlenty and Roger Moe—had each promised me personally that they would rehire staff. It was a promise both uttered during the campaign as well.

I was especially thrilled when Tim Pawlenty won the Governor's race because he had specifically said at the Republican Convention in June that he was going to get the Governor's Residence open and hire the staff back. Candidate Pawlenty also called my home, during all the hoopla, to lend his support.

I saw Governor Pawlenty at the convention myself and asked the then candidate directly what his plans for the former Residence staff were. He apologized for not having enough language in the bill that restored Residence funding to ensure that former staff would be hired back. Then, he took my hand and said, "I look forward to working with you and your staff." That handshake sealed a promise, or so I assumed.

I called many of the former staff to tell them about what Pawlenty had said, and they were as elated as I was. We were eagerly awaiting that invitation back to work after Governor Pawlenty was elected. Instead, we received a letter in the mail saying that the new Governor had found "more qualified" staff to fill our positions. Pawlenty's promise had been the final thin straw of hope that so many of us had been clinging to and, as I read his letter, I felt that straw slip through my fingers.

I almost threw up. That letter was the most dramatic let down I had experienced in a year filled with dramatic letdowns. The impact of Pawlenty's changed position took some time to sink in as I considered how to tell my wife and kids and all the former staff who believed that at last we had found a silver lining, that at last the personal and financial struggles many of us had endured would be over.

All the staff who closed the Residence had scrambled to piece together an income since April 30, and all of us were hindered in our efforts by the public—and our personal—assumption that we would be going back to work at the Governor's Residence soon. Most of us, myself included, took or could only get temporary jobs because every Minnesota employer who interviewed us was under the impression that the Governor would soon be calling and we wouldn't be around for long. I cannot adequately express what this nearly nine-month extension of our misery—of not being able to seek, let alone find, permanent employment—did to our families' financial and emotional health and to our own.

Governor Pawlenty had the opportunity to right a wrong, and he chose to make it worse. I consider Governor Pawlenty's decision not to invite staff back, nor notify them earlier that they would not be coming back, to be the final cruel act against a group of nice, dedicated, hardworking people.

The Residence was a place, and the state of Minnesota an ideal, that we staff loved and served with our hearts and souls as well as our talents, loyalty and dedication. Our efforts deserved more consideration than a kick out the door, a kick in the teeth and a final condescending letter of personal irrelevance.

11

FINAL THOUGHTS

When I went to work at the Governor's Residence in 1999, I was the typical neophyte professional. I was naive, trusting and determined to do and say what was right to serve the state and to serve a man I believed could make that state better. My goal was to serve my Governor and state in whatever way I was needed, and I think that Residence staff and I achieved that goal, and then some, time and again. My only real regret remains not being better able to help the man succeed despite himself.

In nearly every way, my job as Residence manager was the best job I ever had. I put in long hours, but I got to work with superlative professionals and I woke up nearly every morning truly excited to go to the Residence. There was never a dull moment in the public Ventura household, and many of those moments were fun and funny, moving and noble. I treasured watching guests see and appreciate the glory of the Residence as I did every day, and I cherished watching dignitaries, the First Family and their friends truly enjoy an event that staff and I had labored to create. I loved to hear about the good reflection of Minnesota our efforts shone to the state and even the world, and I am proud to know that staff and I contributed something positive to the lasting image of Minnesota.

I'm not so sure that the man I served can ultimately say the same. By the end of Governor Ventura's term, and especially after the mansion closing debacle, many Minnesotans wished they could have "recalled" the memory of their flamboyant gubernatorial experiment.

In 1991, Robert Greenleaf wrote a forceful essay about leadership entitled, *The Servant as Leader*. This short work outlines the concept that a true leader is a servant first, placing the needs of others before his or her own needs are satisfied. Simply stated, a leader "begins with the natural feeling that one wants to serve, to serve first. Then conscious choice brings one to aspire to lead. He is sharply different from the person who is leader first, perhaps because of the need to assuage an unusual power drive or to acquire material possessions."

After the *Playboy* article on Governor Ventura appeared in February 1999, physiologist Aubrey Immelman used a psychological framework to conduct an analysis of the Governor's personality and leader-first leadership style. He concluded that Governor Ventura was a clear-cut example of an autonomous and self-sufficient "dauntless" personality type.

Such people, Immelman noted, "are typically adventurous, fearless and daring, attracted by challenge and undeterred by personal risk. They do things their own way and are willing to take the consequences. Not surprisingly, they often act hastily and spontaneously, failing to plan ahead or heed consequences, making spur-of-the-moment decisions without carefully considering alternatives. This penchant for shooting from the hip—or the mouth—can signify boldness and the courage of one's convictions as easily as it may constitute shortsighted imprudence and poor judgment."

Dauntless personalities, he added, also "often express their impulses directly, often in rash and precipitous fashion and generally without regret or remorse. They rarely refashion their thoughts and actions to fit a socially desired mold." They do, however, often advance social causes, provided the causes somehow advance themselves, Immelman added.

This analysis certainly seems to fit the Governor for whom I worked. He often said that the best thing about being Governor was that "no one can tell me what to do," and that if a bill or issue "affects me then it affects Minnesota," implying that what did not affect Jesse Ventura would not concern Minnesotans. The Governor not only cared little about what others thought of his opinions but also rarely gave but a shrug of consideration to the impact his style might have on a situation such as when he wore a leather jacket to the National Governor's Conference or blue jeans and a sweatshirt to a black-tie state tourism ceremony.

Most significantly to this story is how dauntless personalities react to criticism and problems. Immelman notes that, "when backed into a corner (dauntless personalities) will come out fighting, vowing to get even."

Residence staff are certainly familiar with how well the Governor handles corners. When Governor Ventura backed into the corner he created when he closed the Residence, he fought to keep it closed and kept former staff out regardless, or in complete oblivion, to the personal or political cost to himself or others. As the fight began with the Legislature, it ended with vindictiveness to the staff who once adored him. More than once, the man who promised *Playboy* that he lived "by the Golden Rule: Do onto others as they do onto you," vowed to "get even."

To play the Ventura game the way Jesse would, I suppose I should write this book to remind the Governor that the Golden Rule cuts both ways, inviting others to treat you as you have treated them.

Fortunately for Governor Ventura, I believe in forgiveness, and my goal is to live by the more military-based a code of respect, honor and self-sacrifice that my father taught me. As a citizen "soldier" serving his state and country, much like the soldiers defending it today, I promised myself in 1999 that I would do my job with the Army Code of Conduct in mind, that I would serve Minnesota with:

"Loyalty: to bear true faith and allegiance to the U.S. Constitution, the Army (in my case the state), my unit, and other soldiers; Duty to fulfill my obligations; Respect to treat people as they should be treated, Selfless-Service, to put the welfare of the nation, the state (Army) and my subordinates before my own, Honor to live up to all the (Army) values; Integrity to do what's right, legally and morally; and Personal Courage to face fear, danger or adversity both physical and moral."

I believe I lived up to that Creed in the execution of my public duties as Residence manager. I believe my staff lived up to them as well. I believe in serving a higher value, more than just a serving a boss. I have forgiven the Venturas for falling short of that mantra and am actually appreciative to Governor Ventura for the lessons I learned in serving him, his family and the state of Minnesota. As he is now known for saying, "I'll make you think," Governor Ventura certainly made me think for the past few years!

I thought about the good the Venturas did for the state of Minnesota, and to this day sometimes find myself caught up in the fun and promise—as much as the disappointment and controversy—that was Governor Jesse Ventura. He did much to bring his native state national attention, and he gave a shot in the arm to the idea and hopes of third party candidates nationwide—and to his friend Arnold Schwarzenegger who took the celebrity-governor playbook from Ventura all the way to the California Capitol.

I've thought often about what I could have done differently. I could have said, "yes sir" and "yes madam" at every moment. I could have declined to stand up for my staff when they made mistakes, or when the Venturas misinterpreted their actions. I could have looked the other way as a young man with great potential spiraled out of control and opened the door to danger for himself, the family I cared about and the state of Minnesota.

If I had done those things, I might have fared better in my career with Governor Ventura but I would have been just another political hack. I would not have been the man, and the loyal Minnesota servant, that my family, my staff and my God asks me to be in the face of ethical contravention at the highest levels. I made the choices I did, and wrote this book, because I believe that Minnesotans will be best served by knowing why the Governor's Residence really closed and how easily good and decent people can be trampled by the power and ego of one man or the political machine that drives him.

You did "make me think," Governor Ventura, and after careful consideration, I wouldn't have changed a thing. Well, maybe just one:. I would have petted Franklin more often; he was a good dog.

I I

DAN CREED

Dan Creed is the past executive director of the Minnesota Governor's Residence in St. Paul, serving three and a half years in that post as caretaker and overseer of the state home for Jesse Ventura and his family. As executive director, Mr. Creed supervised 10 full-time and 50 part-time staff, managed a $1 million-plus budget, organized more than 200 events annually, consulted on protocol matters for the Governor and First Lady, supervised remodeling and maintenance of the Residence, and directed Residence public and media relations.

Before going to work for the Ventura administration, the author worked more than 30 years in the business and hospitality fields, including as supervisor of VIP/Guest Services at the Sofitel Hotel in Minneapolis, Minn., and the St. Paul Hotel in St. Paul, where he supervised star treatment for such guests as the Prince of Kuwait, Steven Forbes, Maya Angelou, Peter Graves, Janet Jackson, George

McGovern, Jack Kemp and Bill Murray.

Prior to his hotel experiences, Mr. Creed supervised the GMAC/RFC corporate conference center in Bloomington. He also served as area director for the international nonprofit Ambassador Foundation, where he arranged VIP travel for heads of state, including the Queen of Thailand and King of Belgium, organized conventions for as many as 15,000 people, and spoke on behalf of the foundation in more than 30 foreign countries.

The hospitality expert has a master's degree in organizational management from Concordia University in St. Paul and teaches business, hospitality, hotel management, business ethics and casino management classes at Normandale and Brown colleges in Minnesota. He now serves as director of hospitality outreach for Normandale College.

Mr. Creed also currently serves on the Minnesota Hospitality Human Resources Advisory Board, the United Church of God Advisory Board and the Normandale Hospitality School Advisory Committee. He is treasurer of the Hotel Sales and Marketing Association International Board. He has served on the Central Minnesota Regional Arts Board and the Sower Foundation and Freedom Farm advisory boards and is a past officer of the Family Umbrella Network Board and both the Twin Cities and National Concierge boards. He is also past president of the Montessori School Board.

As a lifetime member of Toastmasters International and the Ambassador Spokesmen Club, Mr. Creed has spoken to groups in Minnesota and in many of the 40 countries and 50 U.S. states he has visited.

A Kentucky native, Mr. Creed attended the University of Kentucky and graduated from Ambassador University in Pasadena, Calif., in 1972, with a bachelor's degree in theology. He worked as manager of the university president's residence and then worked as a family counselor for many years.

His college sweetheart and wife of more than 30 years, Jan, is an educator, who is completing her doctorate in leadership in education. The Creeds have two children, a son and daughter, and live in Elk River, Minn.

| |

ACKNOWLEDGEMENTS

Many people and sources who helped me in writing this book are noted in the resources list below. However, I'd like to take a moment to acknowledge the extra contributions that made this book possible. I thank Diana Pierce at KARE TV who first suggested during an interview that I write this book, and I appreciate the support of my friends, church and community members, students, reporters and even strangers for their support of this endeavor.

I also greatly appreciate the advice and support of my professional coach Mary Sickel, who has mentored and helped me through this process.

Most importantly, I never could I have faced up to or lived through the disappointment thrust upon me without the loving, loyal and steadfast support of my children and my best friend, my wife, Jan. My love and appreciation of you is endless.

I shall always cherish the staff who walked with me down the treacherous path of betrayal and up the other side of hope. May you all find the success and professional contentment you earned and deserve 100-fold, may we always be able to laugh together about all we've been through and may the tears we shed together in the future be only those of joy.

Lastly, and always, I am indebted to the good people of Minnesota for giving me the opportunity to serve them.

II

BIBLIOGRAPHY

American Athiest. (1999, Oct. 2). Ventura Takes Flak, Expands on Religious Remarks. http://www.atheists.org/flash.line/ventura2.htm.

Anderson, Dennis. (Jan. 10, 2003). Ventura Ignored Conservation Woes. *Minneapolis Star Tribune*.

Associated Press. (2002, March 8). Ventura Closes Governor's Mansion.

Associated Press. (2002, Oct. 3). Ventura Didn't Vote in Primary. *Milwaukee Journal Sentinel*.

Associated Press. (2002, Nov. 29). Ventura Era Winds Down in Minnesota. *The Bergen County Record*, N.J.

Associated Press. (2002, Dec. 24). Out of Office, Body and Soul. *Houston Chronicle*.

Associated Press. (2003, Jan. 4). Ventura Warns Media About His Next Act. *Houston Chronicle*.

Bai, Matt and Brauer, David. (1998. Nov. 16). Jesse Ventura's 'Body' Politics. *Newsweek*.

Bai, Matt. (1999, Feb. 15). Ventura's First Round. *Newsweek*.

Bai, Matt. (1999, July 19). Jesse Finds His Big Guy. *Newsweek*.

Bai, Matt (1999, Oct. 25). The Taming of Jesse. *Newsweek*.

Bai, Matt. (2000, June 5). Wrestling for the Center. *Newsweek*.

Bakst, Brian. (2001, Jan. 26). Ventura Asks for Mansion Fix-Up. Associated Press.

Bakst, Brian. (2002, March 8). Governor Says He Will Close Summit Mansion. *St. Paul Pioneer Press*.

Brunswick, Mark. (2002, April 10). Push Is On to Keep Lights On at Governor's Mansion. *St. Paul Pioneer Press*.

Brunswick, Mark (2002, Oct. 2). Ventura Is Among Many Who Don't Go To Polls. *Minneapolis Star Tribune*.

Brunswick, Mark (2002. Nov. 23). Ventura Signs Off, For Now. *Minneapolis Star Tribune*.

Brunswick, Mark. (2003, April 21). Pawlenty Security Tab is Like Ventura's. *Minneapolis Star Tribune*.

Brunswick, Mark. (2003, April 21). Much Attention Paid to Ventura Was Unwanted. *Minneapolis Star Tribune*.

Budig, T.W. (2000, Feb. 5). It's a Personal Vendetta, claims Gov. Ventura About Decision Not to Confirm Minn. *Capitol Roundup*.

Budig, T.W. (2000, May 9). Unicameral Legislature Efforts May Have Flickered Out. *Capitol Roundup*.

Budig. T.W. (2002, May 22). Capitol News. *Elk River Star News & Shopper*. ECM Publishers Inc.

Calvin, Trillin. (2000, Feb. 21). Some Very Interesting Questions. *Time Canada*.

Channel 4000. (1999, Aug. 14). Ventura to Propose Merging Agencies. WCCO TV, St. Paul. http://www.channel4000.com/news/ventura/news-ventura-990814-142009.html.

Channel 4000. (2000, Feb. 3). Moe Says Ventura Appointee Should Resign. WCCO TV, St. Paul. http://www.channel4000.com/news/stories/news-20000203-220036.html.

Channel 4000. (2000, March 10). Unicameral Bill Is On 'Life Support.' WCCO TV, St. Paul. http://www.channel4000.com/news/session2000/news-session2000-20000310-033107.html.

Channel 4000, Associated Press. (2000, May 9). Committee Oks $640 Million in Tax Relief: WCCO TV Reports From the Capitol. WCCO TV, St. Paul. http://www.channel4000.com/news/session2000/news-session2000-20000509-114837.html.

Channel 4000, Associated Press. (2002, March 8). Ventura Closing Mansion Over Budget Flap. WCCO TV, St. Paul. http://www.channel4000.com/msp/news/stories/news-129440620020308-140315.html.

Channel 4000, Associated Press. (2002, Dec. 5). Deficit Reduction Politics Begin in Earnest. WCCO TV, St. Paul. http:/www.bertblyleven.com/msp/news/stories/news-182124220021205-091235.html.

Coffman, Jack, B. (1999, September). Ventura Highway. *American Journalism Review*.

Congress Daily. (2002, July 16). Minn. Independents Endorse Former Lawmaker for Gov.

Conley, Ann and Schultz, David. (2000, Fall). Jesse Ventura and the Brave New World of Politainer Politics. *Journal of American and Comparative Cultures*.

Cooper, Matthew. (1999, Dec. 27). Keeping His Eye on the Ball. *Time*.

Creed, Dan. (1999-2002) Residence Notes.

Creed, Dan. (2001) *How to Operate a Governor's Residence*: A Master's Degree Thesis.

De Fiebre, Conrad. (2000, March 25). Ventura, Legislators Pull No Punches On Air. *Minneapolis Star Tribune*.

De Fiebre, Conrad. (2002, Oct. 23). Ventura's Tour Charms, Chafes. *Minneapolis Star Tribune.*

De Leon, Autumn and Lopez, Steve. (1999, Jan. 18). Ready to Rumble. *Time.*

De Moraes, Lisa. (2003, Feb. 7). Jesse the Body to Become Jesse the Mouth on MSNBC. *The Washington Post.*

De Pree, Max. (1992). Leadership Jazz, p. 227-228. Dell.

Economist, The. (1999, July 24). Right in the Governor's Back Yard. Economist Newspaper Limited.

Economist, The. (1999, Aug. 28). Kiss My Ass. Economist Newspaper Limited.

Economist, The. (2000, Feb. 19). Exit, Pursued by Jesse Ventura. Economist Newspaper Limited.

Economist, The. (2002, May 25). The Ed Who Hopes To Do a Jesse. Economist Newspaper Limited.

Editor & Publisher. Suddenly Silent in St. Paul. (1999, Nov. 27).

Edwards, Tamala, M. (1999, Aug. 9). The Ventura Way: If It Isn't Fun, I Quit. *Time.*

FDCH Political Transcripts. (2002, Oct. 25). Jesse Venura Holds News Conference on Death of Senator Wellstone. eMediaMillWorks Inc.

Fisher, John. (2000, March 4). Bills to Reorganize Department of Commerce Apparently Dead. *Minnesota Legislative News.*

Foer, Franklin and Allen, Jodie. (1999, Sept. 6). The Body, Buchanan, and Beatty. *U.S. News & World Report.*

Freeman, Laurie and Prasso, Sheridan. (2001, Jan. 29). The Body Takes a Blow. *Business Week.*

Furst, Randy. (2002, June 19). Imposter Staged Believable Act at Summit Residence. *Minneapolis Star Tribune.*

Garchik, Leah. (2003, Jan. 9). Jesse Ventura Plots His Path. *SanFrancisco Chronicle.*

Goldberg, Jonah. (2000, Oct. 9). Body Slam. *National Review.*

Grant, Ashley. (2002, Dec. 26). Jesse Stayed True to Self. *Cincinnati Post.* Associated Press.

Grant, Ashley. (2002, Dec. 29). Ventura's Term of Swings. *Milwaukee Journal Sentinel.* Associated Press.

Graubar, Stephen, R. (2001) *Minnesota, Real & Imagined: Essays on the state and its culture.* Minnesota Historical Society Press.

Gray, Paul and Pattison, Kermit. (1998, Nov.16). Body Slam. *Time.*

Greenleaf, Robert. K. (1991). The Servant as Leader, p. 7. The Robert K. Greenleaf Center.

Grow, Doug. (2002, March 17). Watchdog Victimized for Speaking the Truth. *Minneapolis Star Tribune.*

Grow, Doug. (2002, June 6). It's a Pain to Serve at Official Pleasure. *Minneapolis Star Tribune.*

Gustafson, Kristin. (2002, March 24)."Adds Touch of Class to Governor's Home. *St. Cloud Times,* p. 1C.

Henderson, Charles. (99, 10/4). Jesse Ventura's Playboy Interview. www.christianity.about.com/library/weekly/aa100499.htm.

Hinsman, Bill.(1999, June 28). Gov. Jesse Ventura. *Advertising Age.*

Howard, K.C. (2001, Feb. 28). State Budget Forecast Lower Than Initially Expected. Minnesota Daily Online. http://www.daily.umn.edu/ daily/2001/02/08/news/new2/

Howe, Patrick. (2003, June 2). In First Session, Everything Goes Gov. Pawlenty's Way. Associated Press.

Immelman, A. (1999, July 8) Will Jesse "The Adventurer" run for president? It's academia." *Minneapolis Star Tribune,* p. A14.

Jacobson, Louis. (2000, Oct. 28). Getting Beyond Charisma. *National Journal*.

Jones, Tim. (2002, Nov. 19) Ventura Sideshow Readies to Depart Political Midway. Knight Ridder Tribune News Service.

Kavanaugh, John, F. (1999, Oct. 30). Cash, Celebrity and Canned Candidates. *America*. America Press.

Keillor, Garrison. (1999, Oct. 11). Let Jesse Be Jesse. *Time*.

Khoo, Michael. (2001, Feb. 14). Poll: Spend Some of the Surplus. Minnesota Public Radio Web site. http://news.mpr.org/features/200102/14_khoom_poll/index.shtml.

Khoo, Michael. (2002, March 1). Ventura Objects to Budget Cuts. Minnesota Public Radio Web site. http://news.glass.mpr.org/features/200203/01_khoom_budget/index.shtml.

Kriby, David. (1999, May 25). The Body Speaks. *The Advocate*.

Kreiter, Marcella and United Press International. (2002, March 10). Ventura Shutters Mansion. Chicago *Sun-Times*.

Klobuchar, Jim. (1999, May 14). Minnesotans Chortle and Chafe Over Jesse. *Christian Science Monitor*.

Kumar, Kavita. (2002, Aug. 23). Mansion's Doors Swing Open Again. Minneapolis Star Tribune.

Leiby, Richard. (1999, August). I'm Not Like The Other First Ladies'. *Good Housekeeping*.

Legislative Updates. (1999, Jan. 4). First Update. Minnesota State Colleges & Universities.

Legislative Updates. (1999, May 26). Thirteenth Update. Minnesota State Colleges & Universities.

Lentz, Jacob. *Electing Jesse Ventura: A Third-Party Success Story*. Lynne Rienner Publishers. Boulder, Colo. 2002.

Letters From Our Readers. (2000, March 23). The Aitkin Free Press.

Lopez, Patricia. (2003, March 23). Open House at Pawlenty's. *Minneapolis Star Tribune.*

Lopez, Patricia. (2002, April 28). No-longer Affordable Housing. *Minneapolis Star Tribune.*

Lopez, Patricia and Brunswick, Mark. (2002, May 1). Tearful Turn of the Key. *Minneapolis Star Tribune.*

Lopez, Patricia. (2002, May 9). 2 Senators Have Plan to Unlock Mansion. *Minneapolis Star Tribune.*

Lopez, Patricia. (2002, June 4). A Clean Sweep is Planned for Governor's Residence. *Minneapolis Star Tribune.*

Lopez, Patricia. (2002, June 18). 'People's House' or party pad? *Minneapolis Star Tribune.*

Lopez, Patricia. (2002, July 24). A Look Behind Closed Mansion Doors. *Minneapolis Star Tribune.*

Lundy, Walter. (1999, October). Ventura Calls Pioneer Press Writer, Editors 'Bunch of Hypocrites.' *Quill.*

McCallum, Laura. (2000, Feb. 24). Senate Wins Showdown with Ventura. Minnesota Public Radio.

McLaughlin, Abraham. (1999, Sept. 24). Which Governs Better: One House or Two? *Christian Science Monitor.*

McLaughlin, Abraham. (1999, Nov. 5). A Year After Landing, Ventura Leaves Big Political Imprint. *Christian Science Monitor.*

Meier, Peg. (2002, April 28). Governor's Mansion Donor Feels Betrayed. *Minneapolis Star Tribune.*

Meier, Peg. (2002, April 30). Donor Makes a Plea for 'People's Residence.' *Minneapolis Star Tribune.*

Meyers, Mike. (2002, Nov. 26). The Ventura Years. *Minneapolis Star Tribune*

Miller, Kerri. KARE TV News (2002, June 10, 10 p.m.) No Ordinary House Party.

Minneapolis Star Tribune. (2002, Aug. 16). FYI: Governor's Mansion to Reopen Next Week.

Minneapolis Star Tribune. (2002, Nov. 5). Jesse's Pique: There He Goes Again.

Minneapolis Star Tribune. (2002, Dec. 18). Time to Unallot?

Minneapolis Star Tribune. (2002, Dec. 29). The Ventura Years Timeline.

Minneapolis Star Tribune. (2003, Jan. 4). Jesse Ventura: Going Out As He Came In.

Minnesota Legislative Reference Library. (2001, August). Resources on Minnesota Issues: Unicameral Legislature. http://www.leg.state.mn.us/lrl/issues/uni.asp.

Mulroy, Gene, J. (2001, Sept. 4). Jesse Stumps, Gets Body Slammed. *Business News New Jersey.*

National Review. (2002, Nov. 15). The Funeral-Rally. National Review Inc.

Newsweek. (2002. Oct. 7). The Beard & The Body.

O'Connor, Debra. (2001, Jan. 26). Stately Mansion, Needs TLC. St. Paul Pioneer Press.

PBS Documentaries. (2003 accessed). Napoleon at War. *www.pbs.com.*

Penny, Timothy, J. (1999, Sept. 23). Ventura Seriously Defines Reform. *Christian Science Monitor.*

People. (1999, Dec. 31). Jesse Ventura; The gutsy governor's got hold on the country.

People. (2002, July 8). Last Call For Gov. Jesse Ventura–And His Fun-Loving Son Tyrel–The Party Is Over.

Ragsdale, Jim. (2002, May 20). Legislature Shuts Down, Shuts Out Ventura. *St. Paul Pioneer Press.*

Ragsdale, Jim. (2002, June). Ventura Winding Down. *St. Paul Pioneer Press*.

Ragsdale, Jim. (2002, June 19). He'll Walk, Not Run. *St. Paul Pioneer Press*.

Ragsdale, Jim. (2002) Mansion Will Reponen, But Without Old Staff. St. Paul Pioneer Press.

Ragsdale, Jim. (2003, Jan. 3). Ventura's Legacy: In his final year in office, the governor's public support faltered as he waged personal wars. *St. Paul Pioneer Press*.

Reich, Otto. (2002, Sept. 10). Ventura Asks Bush Officials to Apologize. *Congress Daily*.

Rosen, Jill. (2001, December). Media Smackdown! *American Journalism Review*.

Rupp, Myron. *Quotations of Chairman Jesse*. Ruminator Books. St. Paul, Minn. 2002.

Rutenberg, Jim. (2003, June 9). Is He Too Much Muscle for the Medium? *The New York Times*.

Schnayerson, Ben. (2000, Mar/Apr). The Mouth on 'The Body.' *Mother Jones*. Foundation for National Progress.

Schultz, David. (2000, September). Celebrity Politics and Postmodern Political Ethics. *PA Times*. The American Society of Public Administration.

Session Daily. (2000, April 26). News From the House.

Shields, Yvette. (2002, Jan. 11). Ventura, Staring at $1.95B Shortfall. *Bond Buyer*. Thomson Media.

Smith, Dane. (2001, July 14). Ventura has a Hawaiian 5-0 at Governor's Residence Bash. *Minneapolis Star Tribune*.

Smith, Dane (2002, June 23). Ventura's roller-coaster year. *Minneapolis Star Tribune*.

Smith, Dane. (2002, Nov. 24). The Ventura Years: 'Shocking' governor takes stock. *Minneapolis Star Tribune*.

Smith, Dane. (2002, Nov. 26). The Ventura Years: Report card has no A's - and no F's. *Minneapolis Star Tribune*. Nov. 26, 2002.

Smith, Dane. (2002, Dec.1). The Ventura Years Q & A. *Minneapolis Star Tribune*.

Smith, Dane. (2002, Dec. 29). A Term's End, Minnesotans Have Middling View of Governor. *Minneapolis Star Tribune*.

Smith, Dane; et. al. (2002, Dec.29). For Better or Worse: He Rocked Us All. *Minneapolis Star Tribune*.

Smith, Dane (2003, May 7). Ventura and Pawlenty: The Fast and The Curious. *Minneapolis Star Tribune*.

Soucheray, Joe. (2002, March10). Selling Residence Would Pay for Big Guy's Security. *St. Paul Pioneer Press*.

Soucheray, Joe. (2002). Governor of Common Folks Sure Likes Firing Them. *St. Paul Pioneer Press*.

Snyder, Jim. (2000, Feb. 25). Senate Rejects Minn Appointment. *Minnesota Legislative News*.

Sprung, Christopher. (1999, July 16). Jennings Resigns Commerce Post to Take Chamber Position. *Minnesota Legislative News*.

Squitieri, Tom. (2002, June 19). In-Your-Face Gov. Ventura Is Out of Race. *USA Today*.

Squitieri, Tom. (2002, June 20). Ventura's Exit Seen As Blow to Minor Parties. *USA Today*.

Starr, Alexandra. (1999, June). The Man Behind Ventura. *Washington Monthly*.

State Government News. (2000, April). Ventura Leaves Reform Party.

Stein, Joel. (2002, July 1). His Hat is Out of the Ring Too. *Time*.

Sundeen, Ernest R. (1978). *St. Paul's Historic Summit Avenue,* p. 10 – 12. North Central Publishing.

Sweeney, Patrick. (2001, April 18). Costs to Guard Governor up 57%. *St. Paul Pioneer Press.*

Sweeney, Patrick. (2001, Dec. 6). State's Budget Trouble Deepens. *St. Paul Pioneer Press.*

Tieck, Sarah. (2002, January). "Man of the House" *Minnesota Monthly,* p. 43.

Tieck, Sarah. (2003, January). *Minnesota Monthly* magazine, p. 43.

Trouten, Doug. (1999, December). Venturas Comments Draw Strong Reactions. *Minnesota Family Council.*

Uschan, Michael, V. *People In The News: Jesse Ventura.* Lucent Books, San Diego, Calif. 2001.

WCCO TV News. (2000, Feb. 3). Appointment coverage. WCCO TV.

Whereatt, Robert. (1999, March 2).Ventura Has a Private Scolding for Senator Who Criticized His Travels. *Minneapolis Star Tribune.*

Whereatt, Robert. (1999, Aug. 8) Ventura Throws Muscle into Unicameral Request. *Minneapolis Star Tribune.*

Whereatt, Robert, et al. (2000, Feb. 6) Inside Talk: News, Information and Observations. *Minneapolis Star Tribune.*

Whereatt, Robert. (2001, Jan. 26). Mansion Request May Not Find Welcome Mat. *Minneapolis Star Tribune.*

Whereatt, Robert. (2002, Feb. 11). A Tail of Two Rails. *Minneapolis Star Tribune.*

Whereatt, Robert and Lopez, Patricia. (2002, June 19). Ventura Bowing Out. *The Star Tribune.*

Wolfe, Brent. (1999, Aug. 17). A House Divided. Minnesota Public Radio.

PERSONAL INTERVIEWS

Sylvia Sanchez (former Residence administrative assistant) in discussion with author, August 2003.

Cassandra Yarbrough (former Assistant Residence Manager) in discussion with author, August 2003.

Theresa Finnegan (former Residence steward) in discussion with author, August 2003.

Sandy Ellingson (former Residence housekeeper) in discussion with author, August 2003.